MAG NET IC

CULTIVATE CONFIDENCE, BECOME REJECTION-PROOF & NATURALLY ATTRACT THE WOMEN YOU DESIRE

TRIPP KRAMER

To all the men who refuse to remain shy and insecure, may this book transform your life into the confident, charismatic, and attractive man you've always wanted to be.

CONTENTS

PREFACE

I have a memory from when I was five years old. I was at my grandma's house and there was a candy jar filled with colorful, delicious M&M's. To a kid, that's gold. All I wanted to do was eat those suckers up. I stared at them, craving them. They were only two feet away from me. But I was too nervous to grab any. I guess I was afraid my parents would tell me no or I would get yelled at. This was my very first experience of the fear of rejection.

I still have a hard time believing that, as a child, I didn't have the courage to just get some candy. What was the worst that could have happened? My mom says no and then we move on to dinner? Why was I so afraid?

This pattern of shyness continued throughout my childhood, all the way through college and beyond. And it mostly showed up with women and dating. In sixth grade, I had a "girlfriend" (a term I'm using very loosely) named Sara. We were two kids who wrote notes to each other and said we liked each other. After I knew she liked me, I'd ignore her in the hallways and wouldn't speak to her. I was too afraid of what people would think of me. Just a few weeks later, she wrote me a note telling me she thought I didn't like her, and she ended up dumping me. I don't blame her; I barely spoke a word to her because I was too shy.

When I got to high school, I completely blew it again. Somehow, I managed to land one of the cool girls. We were in enough classes together and she thought I was funny. We said we liked each other (this time over AOL Instant Messenger), and then pronounced ourselves a couple.

Just two weeks later, we were sitting in her car and she was waiting for me to give her a kiss. It felt like the M&M's situation all over again. I really wanted to do it, but I was scared. So I gave her a hug, got out of her car, walked upstairs to my room, and got angry with myself. What was wrong with me? Why couldn't I just go for it? A few days later, she ended up telling me she just wanted to be friends. And that was probably because that's exactly how I was acting toward her—as a friend.

I could sit here and write a dozen more stories about how I was too afraid or got rejected, but I think you get the point. My shyness got the best of me for many years, and it didn't allow me to be me. College was the same. I got friend-zoned by many girls. It was embarrassing, to say the least.

After multiple failed attempts with women in college and in my early twenties (and after alcohol-induced attempts with women whom I settled for), I decided to get this part of my life handled. I was determined to do anything I could to meet and attract the women of my choice.

In 2006, I was living in Los Angeles, California, and a buddy of mine was visiting. He told me about a well-known bestseller called *The Game* by Neil Strauss, aka Style, who founded an underground group of pick-up artists. He recounts his personal transformation from dork to ladies' man. When I first read *The Game,* I didn't even really know what a "pick-up artist" was. But I was enchanted with the idea of being able to learn how to meet women.

This book was Pandora's box. It opened up the world of *learning* how to meet women. Growing up, I never thought it was possible to learn that. I thought it was something you either had or didn't. My map of the world said that attractive guys got attractive, quality girls and everyone else got the rest. So I dug deeper.

I started reading every book in sight on dating, attraction, and evolutionary biology. I started learning the skills I might need to attract women. You might be at this point now in your journey. I even joined a group that helped its members become better and more attractive men. With all this new knowledge, I needed to put it to use. I was so eager and dedicated to meeting the type of woman I was really attracted to that I decided to go out three or four times per week and apply all the material I'd learned. At the same time, I was scared shitless. I had to face the fear that had been building up inside of me for years.

It was one of the most interesting times of my life. Over the course of about two years, I met hundreds of women at bars, at clubs, on sidewalks, in grocery stores, at parties, and more. I slept with some. I dated some. I even got into relationships with some. And a lot of these girls were the kind I'd never thought I had a chance with. The crazy thing about this time in my life, when I did "mass approaching," was that it created a new me. I felt more confident in myself. It translated to something bigger than meeting women. I was more outgoing in social situations, less shy with strangers, more assertive at my current job, and less afraid to just be me.

I felt like I'd upgraded to Tripp, version 2.0.

So what was the biggest determining factor of this newfound success? I learned the type of information I needed to get results and then I implemented that information. Simple? Yes. Easy? No. You can learn the proper way to skydive, but once you're in the plane, it's not going to be so easy to jump, right? So what's the missing piece here? What's the one thing that really pushes you to implement and work hard? It's a burning desire to finally be incredible with women and to go after what you want.

Maybe it's the drive to defeat your shyness once and for all.

It could be the fact that you're 22 years old and don't want to have any regrets in your life.

Or it could be that you're 55 and you realize it's time to get what you deserve.

Maybe you see everyone else with your ideal type of woman and you're ready to go after what you want.

For me? I refused to settle for anything less than awesome in my life. I want to call this "drive." Drive is the motivating factor that keeps you going and refuses to give up. And if you want the best results, then you're going to have to dig down deep and find this drive. It's the fuel to the fire of your journey.

Here's a formula to make it easy for you:
Information + Implementation + Drive = Success

Magnetic contains all the information you need to execute this formula. You're going to learn the right information from over 10 years of my experience, success, and mistakes. You're going to learn, step-by-step, how to implement this information so you're not lost in the dark. And I'm going to inspire you to do it.

The strategies, techniques, and instructions in this book can change your life. And that's the main reason why I wrote it. After going through hundreds of rejections and hundreds of successes and finally cracking the code into a simple system to meet and attract quality women, there was no way I could keep this to myself. I wanted all the men like me to learn this, too. And that's why I wrote this book. For you.

It's my mission to help men fix their issues with shyness, dating, and relationships. My job is to help men not only attract women, but also become magnetic. In other words, my job is to show men how to be the guy who naturally attracts women.

Now, how do you know the information in this book is going to get you the women you desire? Honestly, you'll never know until you put the information to use. That's the most powerful proof there is. But to give you some encouragement, I'll let you know the tips and techniques in this book have been tested time and time again. Millions of men around the world have listened to my advice on the Tripp Advice YouTube channel and the "How to Talk to Girls" podcast, and every single day I get emails and messages along these lines:

- I got the girl I thought was out of my league.
- I had an amazing sexual experience with an attractive woman.
- I landed the girlfriend of my dreams.
- I married the best girl.
- I'm dating multiple women at once.

- I'm more confident around my friends, both old and new.
- I found my dream job thanks to assertiveness.

I could go on and on and tell you about the countless men working on turning their lives around from this advice. And I don't say this to show off. I say this to encourage you, the reader, to believe that change is possible and that this stuff works! It doesn't matter what your background is, how much money you have, or if you have an unattractive body and face. The formulas in this book supersede that, which means every guy has a shot. Even you.

So if you're ready to take this journey with me, then let's get started.

Tripp Kramer
Dating Coach for Shy Men

INTRODUCTION

Max is a typical "nice guy." He never wants to rock the boat because he is so afraid of people not liking him. Being accommodating and helpful is always his way of making sure he never had a bruised ego. This results in having friends of both sexes, a well-rounded social life, and lots of opportunities with women. However, because of his fragile ego, he always ends up in the ever-so-common "friend zone." His fear of rejection gets the best of him, so he always decides to befriend girls in hopes they eventually started liking him. Unfortunately, his genius plan doesn't work out, so he never gets more than a hug and told, "I'm sorry. I just don't see you like that. Can we still be friends?" Of course Max will agree to be friends; he still hopes that, one day, any of these pretty girls would see him differently. Little did he know, they never will.

Jon is an asocial, shy kid since the day he was born. He never had any friends in school and focused on his school work. His parents hounded him to get straight A's and focus on his studies. Throughout high school, he had a couple of friends but mainly kept to himself. School was his priority. Years later, in college, he had more opportunities for a social life. People were going out to the bars and there were fraternities to join. But he had absolutely no confidence in being able to make new friends or meet girls. For the next four years, Jon made friends here and there but still stuck to what he knew best: keeping his head in the books. The idea of talking to a girl was scarier than being followed by a man with a white mask and ax. Jon exited college a virgin and entered the real world as an extremely timid person. He craved any sort of sexual attention but resorted to fast-streaming online porn for any feeling of human connection.

Chris is a multimillionaire. He was very successful in his 20s and worked hard to create a business that gave him lavish things and a big condo in the city. Throughout his life, he attracted very beautiful women, but not ones that had much going for them. Instead, they were the types of girls who were attracted to his money more than anything else. Sure, he had women fawning over his Maserati, but rarely would any women actually like Chris for Chris. Most of his relationships were short-lived, superficial, and fake. Women would either sleep with Chris so he could buy them nice things or stick around just long enough to realize his money didn't match his inner confidence. He was too much of a pushover, and that sent them searching for a more secure man.

Steve is an incredibly attractive and charming guy. In fact, in high school he did very well for himself. He was the most popular kid in school and lost his virginity at age 15. His confidence was rock solid for quite a long time until he reached his early 20s, when something weird happened. He lost touch with his ability to socialize with women. In his younger years, women would come up to him because he was known as the "cool guy."

But now, being in the real world, things were different. Steve realized he had to be the one to approach women and start conversations, and this idea seemed kind of difficult. In his mid-20s, Steve, although still a handsome guy, rarely goes on dates because he just doesn't know how to interact with women in a way that gets them interested.

Then there is Pete. He is 43 and recently divorced. He'd married his high-school sweetheart, and after 15 years of marriage he was back on the dating market. Now that there are online dating apps, he has no idea where to start. He's already passed his prime and has no idea what kind of women are out there. Should he start an online dating profile? Should he talk to girls at loud clubs? All these ideas seem miserable to him, so he sits alone on Friday night and eats Chinese food, watches Netflix, and feels a deep void, all of which results in painful loneliness.

These are the kinds of guys I hear about every single day. And maybe you can relate. Sure, it might not be your exact situation, but I bet you see a side of yourself in Max, Jon, Chris, Steve, and Pete. Besides the names, these are real men I've coached to get their dating lives back in order.

In some shape or form, these are the problems I hear all the time. Most guys

- don't know what to say to girls
- can't approach a girl due to fear
- aren't sure how to keep a girl around once they're initially interested
- can't get a girl to want to have sex with them
- get a girl's number but she doesn't respond
- end up in the friend zone with a girl they were obsessed with
- can't get past hello in a conversation

If you're nodding your head yes to any of these, then you've come to the right place. Meeting and sleeping with girls, attracting those seemingly untouchable girls out of your league, and having a dating life filled with amazing, sexy women is what many men desire and most men don't achieve. Why? Because they don't have the right information. Either that or they sit in "analysis paralysis," which means they don't know where to start due to an overload of information from books and the Internet.

In the following chapters you're going to discover a proven system that takes you from steps A–Z on how to meet, attract, and seduce beautiful women. It doesn't matter what your background is, how much money you have, or what you look like. If you follow the techniques in this book, you'll become what I call a Magnetic Man—a guy that draws women toward him.

Now, let's talk about hard work for a second. The reality of life is that when you want something you have to work at it. However, with the right information you can sometimes cut that work in half. For example, let's say you wanted to learn how to run long distance so you could get a good time for a full marathon. The bottom line is, you're going to have to do a lot of running, which requires a lot of effort. But let's say you start training and you have a crappy pair of shoes or even the wrong type of shoes for running. These shoes are going to cause your feet to swell up and make your ankles sore. They're going to slow you down because they don't have the right tread. These bad shoes are going to make the work for you much harder.

Now, let's say you did some research and got the right running shoes. They have great support for your feet, the correct bottom tread for long-distance running, and the right fit. You just saved yourself a ton of work. No more icing your ankles when you come home. No more wasted energy by pushing harder against the pavement.

Consider this book your brand-new pair of running shoes. Are you going to have to put in work and complete some exercises and action steps? Yes. Will you be challenging yourself to become version 2.0 of you? Absolutely. But the good news is, you're going to have guidance, direction, and a roadmap, so you'll complete the goal faster. And the goal here is to become magnetic to the types of women you desire.

I've helped millions of guys just like you get the women they want. This book is 10 years of expertise condensed down to a simple system. I'm going to need you to buckle down with me and put faith in something that works. If you follow my direction and take this journey seriously, then you'll enter a secret, highly exclusive club of men. The only people who have the key to this club are the guys who step up and say, "Let's get to work."

You're going to need something called resilience. Resilience is the capacity to recover quickly from difficulties. I'm not going to beat around the bush. Some of the action steps described in this book will be challenging. Others are going to be super easy. It's different for every guy. You may find yourself saying something like this:

"Do I really have to do that?"

"Wait, what if she rejects me?"

"That's not something I could *ever* do!"

"Is this absolutely necessary?"

Or those thoughts won't come up at all. The point is, the good things in life can be hard to obtain. But they're *not* impossible. I promise this book will make picking up girls as easy as possible—but only to a point. You'll eventually have to put this book down, talk to girls, and create movement in your life. But I'm on your side, every step of the way.

All I ask is that you come back to this idea of resilience. When things get hard or you feel stuck or defeated, pull yourself back up and keep going. Many moments in my life have been this way, but I still kept going despite the challenge and came out clean on the other side.

I remember the first night I ever went out to meet women. I was out for a total of four hours. It felt like an eternity. The goal of the night was to talk to at least a few women. By the end of the night I talked to a whopping total of zero. Four hours and I couldn't even say hi to a woman. It was miserable. I came home completely defeated. All I was trying to do was speak words to the opposite sex. This wasn't rocket science! Still, it was incredibly hard and I wanted to give up right then and there. But then something hit me. I had two options. Option A: I could give up and settle for any girl that would give me the time of day, and I could be miserable about it. Option B: I could continue working hard at this and either end up in the same place as Option A or end up succeeding.

Looking at it that way, I realized that Option B was clearly the better choice because I had nothing to lose. And neither do you. If you decide *not* to treat this book as a guide, then you'll be in exactly the same place. But if you decide to work through it, then you can attract some of the most gorgeous women on the planet.

So let's work hard, practice resilience, and start implementing. Deal?

First, let's go over what's in this book and how to use it for optimal results.

WHAT DOES THIS BOOK COVER AND HOW DO YOU USE IT?

Simply put, I'm going to teach you the following:
1. How attraction works (what makes a woman want a man)
2. How you trigger attraction (how to be the man that women want)
3. How you make attraction last (how to create the relationship you desire)

There are 9 chapters, which will give you mindsets, practical exercises, and techniques you can use to implement the information. My strong suggestion is that you *do not* skip ahead and read future chapters without reading the previous ones. While each chapter does stand on its own, it's more beneficial to have read earlier chapters for the context of earlier lessons.

Ideally, you want to read one chapter at a time and don't go to the next chapter until you've completed all the exercises and action steps. That way, you'll be fully ready for the next learning lesson and its accompanied assignments. It's like a textbook for school: you'll understand and get more out of each following chapter once you've learned the previous one.

There might be some concepts you've heard before. Great! Hearing and learning things more than once helps you retain the information better. You're also going to learn some things that might question your reality. Even better. I want to challenge your way of thinking so we get down to the truth of how dating, attraction, and sex really work. Of course, you can question anything I discuss in this book and shouldn't ever blindly believe something. It's your job to take questionable information and test it.

When I tell you to say a specific line to a girl, go out and use it. See if it works for you. But remember, don't give up if something doesn't work once. Remember what I said earlier about resilience. Try things over and over again. Put all the concepts you learn together. Take action on the exercises and try things again and again until you succeed. This information has been tested, so with enough time and work, it should work for you, too.

On another note, unless stated otherwise, the techniques described in this book are geared toward meeting a woman in-person and for the first time. While some of the information can help you attract a girl you already know or are in the friend zone with, it's more useful for first-time "approaches," also known as "cold approaches." It's best to use this information for in-person, first-time interactions.

A NOTE ON MEN AND WOMEN

Over my 10 years of being a dating coach, I've found a lot of guys complaining about how they have to do all the work. You might start reading this book and halfway through think, "Wow, there's a lot of things a guy has to do to trigger attraction. Where's the woman's role in this? How come I have to do everything?"

That's a fantastic question. It does appear that men are the ones approaching, starting conversation, leading them to the bedroom, getting on one knee, etc. First, what you have to understand is that this is how nature intended it. The male peacock spreads its feathers to impress the female peacock. The male hummingbird moves from side to side in a dance fashion to court the female hummingbird. The list goes on.

In Chapter 1, you'll learn about the human traits that attract a female, and one of those is dominance. This means that you are the one who is leading. The actual act of you approaching and making the first move *is* what attracts her. So remember that she's not lazy; she's just waiting for a masculine, dominant man to show up.

Also, what most guys don't realize is that women have a job, too. It's her job to display her feminine traits to get you interested! The reason you want to talk to her in the first place is because you find her physically attractive. She's doing her part to look that way and attract you. She's getting her nails and hair done, spending time getting ready. Not to mention the danger she faces interacting with a man, due to high instances of assault.

And once you go talk to her, she's displaying her personality as well. So it really does take two to tango in the game of attraction. And if you don't think the woman is working on her part, then go to your nearest bookstore and check out the self-help section. You'll see shelves of books on dating advice for women. They're working on it, too.

Either way, the big idea is to know *how* to attract women and *be the man* that attracts women. So if you're ready, then let's head to the next chapter, where we'll learn the principles of attraction and what will turn you into a Magnetic Man.

— ∾ —

CHAPTER 1

HOW TO ATTRACT A WOMAN WITH 3 EFFORTLESS TECHNIQUES

Remember Max? He was one of the first examples from the Introduction. If you haven't read the introduction, then I suggest you get right to it. (This is your first lesson to not skip ahead!)

So Max was labeled as the "nice guy." The poor fella couldn't get a girl to like him if his life depended on it. He went through what I call the "back door" to try to get girls interested. The back door goes something like this:

Well if I meet a girl and get her to spend as much time with me as possible, then eventually she'll like me. And I'm too afraid of rejection, so I won't try and make any moves whatsoever. Eventually, she'll come around and see what a nice guy I am, since we're friends, and one day she'll fall in love with me.

Unfortunately, this is not how attraction works, and it's also a massive waste of time.

> **Your job is to display masculine qualities and show her you are a potential mate, not a friend.**

In this chapter, we'll go over what those masculine qualities are and how you can display them when you meet her. But first, you need to understand more of the theory behind how attraction works.

Let's break down the qualities of every man. There are inner qualities and outer qualities. Inner qualities are your personality traits such as open-mindedness, courage, dependability, and politeness. Outer qualities are your looks, income, and lifestyle.

Understand this: women are hard-wired to respond to a man's inner qualities (his personality) more than his outer qualities. A man's personality traits are what tell a woman if she should have sex with him and reproduce. She needs to know she's with a man who possesses certain masculine qualities so her children will be healthy and survive. Let's quickly take a dive into prehistoric times.

According to theories in evolutionary psychology, women are more attracted to intangible personality traits such as ambition, courage, and assertiveness because these characteristics are associated with men's access to resources. In caveman times, women who mated with men of resources ensured their children's survival.

On the other hand, it's a little different for a man's attraction to a woman. You are initially attracted to her outer female traits such as waist proportions, breast shape, skin clarity, hair thickness, and youth, because these signal healthy reproductive capabilities. These feminine traits are symbols of a healthy woman who will bear healthy children. And then, after you get to know her, you'll look for her personality traits as well: nurture, warmth, sensitivity, and intelligence.

You may be wondering, "But I usually just see beautiful women with the typical good-looking guys. How can personality make such a big difference?"

Here's the deal with that. Yes, physical attraction will attract a woman. Leonardo DiCaprio can walk into a room and probably have any girl he wants. However, what you don't realize is that it's his fame and looks that get his foot in the door. Mr. DiCaprio has a lot of other things going for him: talent, charisma, success, and communication skills. Average guys will see Leonardo DiCaprio picking up a girl and only think it has to do with this looks. Why? Because that's how attraction works for men. The truth is, personality traits (inner qualities) carry more weight than looks.

On the other hand, if I had a dollar for every time I heard a story about a high-quality girl going on a date with a typical, strong, square-jawed fella only for her to never see him again, I'd be rich. That's because he was a dud. Conversation was boring and he was more of a shell than anything else. I also hear plenty of stories about women dating men that are short, chubby, and balding, yet they fall in love. Why? Because, those guys had charm, intelligence, and personality. Personality will always be the deciding factor. Remember, it's what women are wired to be attracted to; they're attracted to the inner qualities.

My point so far is that looks, money, height, age, and penis size do *not* determine a woman's attraction to a man. Your best bet is focusing on how to build your social skills and charisma (inner qualities) while working on your outer qualities in the background (which we will discuss more in Chapter 2).

Another point is that you're in some heavy competition, my friend, if you only focus on your outer qualities. That's what every other guy in the world who doesn't know the truth is doing. They go to the gym obsessively and show off their money to women, which, let's be honest, takes a lot of work. But your personality is unique. And you have a much better chance of using your unique personality to attract women than scraping up dollars to rent a Lamborghini for a day.

ATTRACTION IS AN EMOTIONAL REACTION

Imagine you see a beautiful girl walking down the street. She's just your type. For many guys, that's long smooth legs, a busty chest, long flowing hair, and a perfect smile. Picture it for a moment. What's happening inside your body? You get a nice warm feeling, don't you? That's attraction. She's exhibiting many of the healthy feminine qualities we discussed earlier. Your primal instinct is to mate with her because you see a very fertile woman. The reaction is almost instant. If she came up to you on the street and asked to sleep with you (assuming it wasn't a prank), I bet you wouldn't hesitate for a second.

For a woman, it's much different. She doesn't get turned on as quickly. I stated earlier that women are more attracted to your inner qualities—your personality. How fast do you think you can show a girl your personality? Well, she can't get a sense of it until she meets you, so it's not going to happen from across the room. It's up to you to approach her and start conversation, and once you're talking to her, it could take anywhere from 30 minutes to a few hours for you to display your attractive personality traits. We'll be going over the most powerful traits soon, but understand that it takes much longer for a woman to decide if she wants to sleep with you. It's not as instant as it is for you.

I credit David DeAngelo, famous dating coach, when he said, "Attraction is not a choice." You don't choose to be attracted to somebody. It happens on a primal, biological level. It's an emotional reaction. The good news is, you can tap into this even if you're not a physically attractive guy. When you display masculine personality traits, you can trigger her attraction for you. Let's go over what those are right now.

THE 3 PRINCIPLES OF ATTRACTION

Now that we understand how attraction works, I want to teach you how to trigger it when you're with a woman. I call them "principles" because they're the foundation of what makes a woman attracted to you. These principles have shown up, in one form or another, in every interaction throughout history when two people had sex or formed a relationship.

These principles are masculine personality traits, and that's why they work in triggering attraction. The three principles are tension (T), entertainment (E), and dominance (D), also known as TED. When you display these traits, you exponentially increase your chance of triggering attraction. Most guys fail to display these traits and either end up in the friend zone or get rejected. Using these foundational principles gets her thinking about you as a potential mate.

CREATING SEXUAL TENSION

Let's start with T, which stands for "tension." Most guys choose to ignore this one when interacting with women. Tension results from a woman feeling the presence of masculinity. It's the same feeling you get when you're talking to a girl and *you* say to yourself, "I think she likes me." If you've never had that feeling, then let's say it's similar to the feeling of being turned on or horny around a woman.

When a woman feels that same way, there's sexual tension between you two. The idea here is to create that when you're with her. One of the simplest ways to do that is with eye contact, body language, and vocal tonality, which are aspects of nonverbal communication. When you're in the presence of a woman, the way you carry yourself speaks volumes and has the capacity to create massive sexual tension.

Eye Contact. When you meet a girl for the first time or you're on a date, you want to give her consistent eye contact. Most guys don't do this right. You want to be looking her directly in the eyes when you speak to her. If you're having trouble, one trick is to look at her in one eye and focus on that. It's much easier and still comes across like you're looking in both eyes.

Eye contact creates tension because it shows her you're interested, engaged, and courageous. One of the signs of shyness or social anxiety is not being able to look at someone in the eyes. When you can comfortably look at a woman's eyes, you show her you're not nervous. This is very attractive to her. Your confidence, courage, and ability to show her you're taking action demonstrate your mental strength (an inner quality).

Body Language. When you're in conversation with a woman, I want you to be facing her, shoulder to shoulder. Imagine standing directly in front of a mirror. Now pretend you're looking at yourself. That's exactly how you need to stand to create tension. Most guys won't be as direct, and they'll stand off to the side (Figure 1) or stand at a 45-degree angle (Figure 2). Instead, mirror her (Figure 3) so she can feel your presence.

Figure 1

Figure 2

Figure 3

Vocal Tonality. As a confident man, you should be speaking in a way that makes you sound sure of yourself. You want to communicate that to a woman by using the tone of your voice. Women have told me they're turned on just by hearing the sound of a man's voice! It's powerful stuff. The way in which you want to communicate is in "downward tonality."

The best example of downward tonality is the way in which you'd talk to a dog. Let's say you were telling your dog nicely to come to you. Imagine how you would say it:

"Here, boy! Come, boy! Good boyyyy. C'monnn, boy!"

Your voice would go up in inflection and the pitch would move higher.

On the other hand, imagine if you were disciplining a dog because he just peed on your new rug. You might yell and say something like this:

"Hey, get over here! You're a bad dog. Very bad dog. Don't you ever do that again!"

Imagine how your voice sounds when you say that. It would have a lower inflection and go a bit deeper. Your voice is more demanding, more certain, and more direct—all very masculine traits. When you're with a woman, however, you aren't yelling at her, so don't take this example too literally. Instead, speak to her so your tonality is firmer and goes down at the end of your sentence.

Eye contact, body language, and vocal tonality can be very powerful in creating sexual tension. You're displaying your masculinity by showing her you're not afraid, which in turn makes you appear more confident. The secret here is that your nonverbal communication has a massive effect on your inner confidence. When you work on playing the role as a confident person, you'll feel more confident.

You can also create sexual tension with your words. More on that in Chapter 3 where we discuss flirting.

PROVIDING ENTERTAINMENT

The second principle of attraction is providing entertainment. This concept is very counterintuitive and most guys mess it up. When you're talking to a girl, it's not about entertaining her; it's about entertaining *yourself*. In an interaction where you're trying to prioritize the way *you* feel, you'll end up bringing her into your world instead of trying to be part of hers. This shows that you're not needy, which is an unattractive trait. Let's go deeper, because you need to understand the subtle implications this has on a conversation with her and people in general.

According to the law of state transfer, when you're in a certain mood, you can easily transfer that mood over to someone else. We as human beings are very susceptible to another person's emotions. We're hardwired to build connections with the people we communicate with, so we can easily take on what they're feeling. Don't believe me? Let me illustrate a few examples.

Have you ever been around a friend who drags you down? They're always negative and talking about how much their life sucks. How do you feel after spending just 30 minutes with them? Kind of crappy, right?

How about when you're with someone who's having fun and making jokes? At the worst, maybe you're not laughing with them, but you're definitely feeling a little lighter since you're surrounded by a positive state.

Have you ever had a homeless person walk up to you and say something crazy? You probably feel a little uncomfortable just being in their presence. That's because they're transferring their unstable energy to you. And it can happen almost instantly!

Tony Robbins, a famous motivational speaker, has his audience get up, dance, and scream at the top of their lungs several times at his big events. That's because he's getting everyone into a state of joy, freedom, and happiness. Having all that crazy energy around puts you in a great mood.

What does this have to do with providing entertainment for yourself when you talk to women? When you prioritize the way you feel, it can carry over to the way *she* feels. Imagine walking up to a girl at a bar. Now imagine you've got a big frown on your face, your hands are in your pockets, and you're shaking as you're talking to her. Right away, she's going to start feeling anxious because she's in the presence of nervousness. So let's do the opposite. Let's approach girls with a big smile and big energy.

For one, it's going to take practice. I understand that you may be afraid of approaching a beautiful woman at the bar or on the street, so just remember that it's okay if you don't immediately get this right. It's something you hone in on over time.

The keyword here is "silly." I want you to think of something that's silly to you. Acting silly or doing something silly will be fun for you, entertain you, and therefore create a light-hearted and fun interaction with a woman. I want to be very clear here: it has to be fun for *you*. If it's not, then we're back to trying to entertain and get something from her. That's the opposite of what we're going for. Here are some examples of things that are silly, but only steal these if they resonate with you. Otherwise, you can come up with your own:

- Teasing the girl you're talking to by calling her a dork
- Grabbing her hands for a second and dancing with her when a new song comes on
- Saying an inside joke you have with another friend
- Narrate out loud what you think she's thinking in the moment
- Call her out on something she likes or dislikes
- Thumb-wrestling with her

These are examples of being silly. The sky's the limit here. The mindset is about finding something that's funny or fun to you and using that in your interactions with women. Another mindset is the idea of curiosity. Use curiosity to your benefit by experimenting and seeing what could be interesting, funny, or silly to you in an interaction.

When you're having this much fun with yourself, you're displaying a personality of a fun-loving, charismatic, and confident person. These traits communicate that you're a provider and protector. Your ability to be charismatic and confident signals to her on a biological level that you "have life handled," which means you can provide resources for a healthy family. You may be thinking, "All from being silly and fun in an interaction?" Yes. Remember, displaying your inner qualities is what turns her on.

On top of that, your ability to entertain yourself says that you're not outcome-dependent. This means that you aren't worried about what she thinks and that you're not trying to get something from her. Most beautiful and quality women have men trying to get something from them: sex. Yet these men don't know how to do it, so they try to "entertain" her by asking her 100 questions and trying to get her to do all the work. This appears desperate and needy. When a woman knows you don't *need* her, she sees your inner strength. And this also adds an element of mystery to you because she's interacting with a man who's so carefree.

DISPLAYING DOMINANCE

The third principle of attraction is dominance, and the best part about dominance is that it kills two birds with one stone. Dominance helps you move an interaction toward sex while also displaying your masculinity.

A synonym for dominance is control. One of the most common mistakes I see guys make is that they're not in control of the interaction. Most guys have absolutely no plan when they see or meet a girl they're interested in. For a clueless guy, his map is this:

1. See girl
2. Think of something to say
3. Say it
4. Hope she wants to have sex with him
5. Maybe sex happens and she likes him

To be brutally honest, I might even be giving a guy too much credit here. It might be something like this:

1. See girl
2. Think of something to say
3. Say it
4. Hope one day he can see her again

This is a rough map and not the way to properly learn how to meet and attract a woman. There has to be a plan so you can get to the end goal. That's how you become successful at anything: by having a goal.

Stephen Covey, author of *7 Habits of Highly Effective People*, talked about it best when he said to "start with the end in mind." Your end in mind here is sex, because sex is the biggest form of investment a woman can make (more on this in Chapter 6) and keeps you out of the friend zone. Of course, your goal might also be to see if she's a potential partner for a relationship. If that's the case, you'll learn about how to incorporate this into your interactions in Chapter 8.

For now, let's understand that your job as a man is to move the interaction toward sex and beyond. She will not do it for you. I repeat: she will not do it for you. That's not a woman's job in the mating dance—it's yours. She'll be attracted to you when she knows you can lead from beginning to end.

You may have some specific how-to questions, such as what to say and how to lead her to the bedroom. Those answers will come as we continue through the chapters, but first, let's discuss the general idea of how to get from Point A (hello) to Point B (sex and relationship).

THE APPROACH

When you see a girl you want to talk to, your objective is to talk to her, right? So you need to focus on *that* being the first goal. You need to beeline toward her and start conversation (more specifics on this in Chapter 3). Most guys will hesitate to go over and talk to her and wait for "the right time." The right time to talk to a girl is always *now*. There are very few exceptions to this rule. The longer you hesitate, the more you'll feel scared and the more chances you have to convince yourself to *not* do it. Use the three-second rule and approach a girl within three seconds of seeing her to get the job done before your brain convinces you not to.

THE BOUNCE

Next, once you're in conversation, your goal is not to get her number. That's what most guys think, but that's actually the backup plan. Remember, your overarching goal here is to eventually have sex with her. This is what separates friends from lovers. So when you're talking to her at a bar, on a sidewalk, at an event, or in a grocery store, your objective is to bounce to another location. That could be going for coffee, grabbing food, or going to your place, for example. Keep this in mind as you're interacting with her.

THE NUMBER

Now, it's not possible in all scenarios to continue seeing her right after your first interaction. Logistics might not favor continuously hanging out. Or maybe she doesn't feel enough trust to continue hanging out. In that case, you'll want to get her number so you can see her again in the future.

THE DATE

This is the part most guys screw up. A lot of guys get a girl's number and text all kinds of random messages and never ask her on a date. Remember to focus on the goal, and right now your goal is to get her to meet up with you in person. You'll learn how to arrange meeting up with a girl via text in Chapter 5.

SEX

Once you're on the date, your next goal is to lead her into the bedroom. It's important to make sure you're physically escalating to the point where she desires to have sex with you. More on this in Chapter 7.

SECOND DATE

Of course, sex may not happen on the first date. Then you're going to want to see her for a second time, so you'll go back to the part where you text her and arrange another date.

I understand that a lot of this information sounds extremely calculated and robotic at times, as if we're only focused on getting to sex as quickly as possible. What you have to understand is that the biggest difference between the relationship you have with your friends and family and the one you have with a woman you like is sex. That's the underlying tension that exists between you and her in this courting process. In between the times you're focused on the goal, you're still getting to know her on a personal level and connecting with her, but I want you to be mindful that sex might never happen if you don't focus on the aforementioned goals of leading the interaction. And if you're moving too slowly, it's very possible for another guy to swoop in while you get thrown into the friend zone.

Dominance is leading the interaction from hello to sex. The reason *she* doesn't do it is because a woman's primal desire is to be led. She gets turned on and attracted when a guy is creating a safe and open space for her to be sexual. The masculine penetrates, and the feminine receives. The masculine is dominant while the feminine is submissive. You need to bring your assertiveness to the table and take the lead from beginning to end.

APPLYING THE 3 PRINCIPLES OF ATTRACTION

It's important to understand that tension, entertainment, and dominance are not supposed to be structured in a linear fashion. It's not about building tension and then providing entertainment and then being dominant and leading the interaction. Instead, it's about applying these principles throughout the course of an entire interaction. If this sounds overwhelming, don't worry, I will teach you step-by-step how to put it all together in easy action steps.

You'll build sexual tension by using nonverbal techniques while at the same time providing your own entertainment and consistently leading the interaction.

Is that it? Just work on these three principles and a girl will fall into your arms? No, not necessarily. You still have to learn some of the nuances, such as continuing conversation, flirting (which helps build sexual tension), and setting up the date. We will get into that in the following chapters.

However, practicing *only* these three principles and having no other skills will get you very far in your ability to seduce women. Even though you may not feel confident with women, just applying these techniques will make you appear more confident than 90 percent of the guys who've ever tried (or not tried) talking to her.

To make it easy for yourself, you can take each principle and practice it on its own when you're talking to girls. And then, when you've got it down, you can use all three. My suggestion is to start with tension because I believe it's the most straightforward. Make it a goal to go up and talk to women at a bar or public place. Walk straight up to them and say, "Hi, I saw you over here and you look nice." Make sure you're facing her, giving her eye contact, and talking in the correct tonality. Remember, the objective here isn't to sleep with her or get her number. The objective is practicing tension. If you do 20–30 approaches in a week, you'll have tension down cold. Just by the odds, you'll probably end up getting a few phone numbers.

Next, I'd focus on entertainment. Think of something you find funny, interesting, or silly. You can use some of the previous examples *only* if they feel funny or silly to you. Even better, come up with something of your own. There's no right or wrong here. The judgment is up to you, not her. We're not entertaining her. We're creating our own fun, which will then transfer over to her. Take another week or two and just focus on talking to girls while applying this entertainment principle. Watch how fun interacting with women becomes and see how much it lets her guard down—and yours, for that matter.

Last, focus on dominance. Make it a habit to try and continue hanging out with a girl after the initial interaction. If you meet her at a bar, get her to come with you to another bar or say you have a good bottle of wine back at your place. Don't worry if you get rejected! The objective is to apply the principle. If she doesn't want to continue hanging out, get her number. From there, don't forget to text her and get her on a date. We'll discuss this more in Chapter 5, but do your best for now. Think progress over perfection. On the date, try and end up back at your place by telling her you have some good snacks or a nice bottle of wine. Otherwise, you can just use something from your conversation related to bringing her back to your place. An example might be listening to a vinyl record of a band you both liked.

For a week or two, only focus on dominance and push the interaction toward sex. This does *not* mean being forceful with women. If they don't want to have sex or get physical with you, then it stops there. It's important to get consent from a woman before sex. More on that in Chapter 6.

2 TRAITS THAT TURN WOMEN OFF

Two traits can turn women off: neediness and predictability. I want to teach you about how to avoid these two traits so your interactions go smoothly and she wants to keep seeing you. If you display these traits, you'll cancel out the three principles and make it harder for her to be attracted to you.

First, let's talk about neediness. Ensure you're not trying to "get" anything from her. It's a difficult mentality to have because lots of guys are in the mindset of "get" or "take." They want to "get" her number, *not* "get" rejected, "get" a date, or "get" sex. This is very low-value thinking and can get you into a lot of trouble.

The moment you become needy, you end up "getting" less. That's because a woman doesn't want to be with a man who has a lack of resources. And no, I'm not talking about money; I'm referring to the primal sense of being able to care for oneself. Your ability to provide for yourself, with no desperation, illustrates that.

Neediness is also emotionally unhealthy. It says you aren't good enough to stand on your own and reinforces the idea that women are to be used for something. Women are amazing creatures with beauty inside and out. Let's not try to ever get something from them. Instead, let's be magnetic and pull women toward us by displaying our masculine qualities.

How do we avoid being needy? Entertainment will be very helpful in this area. Go into every interaction while asking how you can make it fun and enjoyable for yourself. Ask yourself these following questions:

"What can I talk about that's interesting to *me*?"
"What makes *me* feel entertained and happy?"
"How can I bring her into *my* fun world?"

A good start is by being silly, like I discussed above. Another way is to talk about things you want to talk about and seeing how she responds. Talk about the things you like, such as music, the interesting things you've heard in the news, your opinions on the latest Quentin Tarantino flick, or why you'll never go bungee jumping. The topics you're interested in offer up interesting conversation because *you* are interested in them, which makes you less needy and gather entertainment from *her*.

Another thing I want to add is the idea of abundance mentality. This mindset reinforces that if it doesn't work out with one woman, then another one is around the corner. A good technique is to act like 100 women are texting you at once. Let's imagine that you literally have 100 women texting you to meet up. How would you act in this situation? Well, it won't be possible to meet every single one. Some women you'll respond to, some you won't, and some you'll just plain forget about. If you're setting up a date with a woman and you have 99 other girls to choose from, do you think you'll be texting her nonstop to meet up or desperately thinking of ways for her to choose you? You won't. You'll just move on to the next girl. Every woman is unique. There's another one right around the corner if things don't work out. And that's a fact.

From this new mindset, you'll never have to be needy or try to "get" anything from a woman. To practice abundance, you'll need to meet as many women as you can so you truly understand the number of women there are in the world. From here, you won't feel as heartbroken when it doesn't work out with one.

The second unattractive trait is predictability. Being predictable means you're engaging with her logically instead of emotionally. Most men will engage logically with a woman. They say things like "What do you do for work?" or "Do you come to this bar often?" or "What's your favorite cereal?" They talk to women like it's an interview process and they're just trying to grab the facts. Not only is this trying to "get" something from her, as I explained with neediness, but it's also not hitting her emotionally. Attraction happens at an emotional level, not a logical one. If she's bored, she won't be attracted, and predictability breeds boredom.

Here's the good news: this book is going to continually lay out techniques and applications to make sure you're not some average Joe. However, to start being unpredictable, you can follow the three attraction principles laid out thus far. They all help instill emotion in her because you're building attraction. The tension techniques help you build sexual tension and treat her like she's a potential mate and not a friend. Providing entertainment is huge in unpredictability because it engages with her in a way that makes it interesting. Dominance helps move the interaction forward by continuously building tension but also letting her know you're a man that can provide amazing sex.

Below is the first set of action steps I want you to take to put this information into practice and start getting results. One of the first steps is to read the section in Chapter 2 on approach anxiety, just in case going up to women is difficult for you. It's the only time I'll ask you to jump ahead in the book. I understand how debilitating it can be to talk to a new woman for the first time. Just remember, you can overcome approach anxiety by approaching more and more women. It's a very annoying catch-22, but it's the reality of the situation. Hint: baby steps make this process easier.

Get ready for Chapter 2, where I'll teach you how to be a guy that women want to talk to and how to build the lifestyle women crave.

ACTION STEPS:

- Read the section titled "How to Defeat Approach Anxiety and Shyness Around Girls" in Chapter 2, and practice Steps 1–8 (you'll see what I'm talking about after you read it).

- Go to http://www.trippadvice.com/chick-crack/ and download a free video that talks about the topics of conversation that women love.

- Practice by walking by a woman, smiling, and not breaking eye contact until she does. Do this three times.

- Approach one woman and practice mirroring body language saying the line, "Hi, I saw you over here and you look nice. Are you from [insert city you live in]?"

- Think of something funny or silly and provide entertainment for yourself. Try using this with one woman you approach.

— ∼ —

CHAPTER 2:

HOW TO MAKE WOMEN APPROACH YOU (USING MY 4-STEP ATTRACTION AMPLIFIER)

W hen I was growing up, there was a show on television called *Saved by the Bell.* I used to love this show. It was one of the most popular shows for kids growing up in the '90s. If you haven't seen it, then I'll give you a little breakdown. It's about a group of six friends in high school who get into all kinds of random adventures. On the show you have Zack Morris, a good-looking popular kid, and his best friend Screech, the biggest nerd in school. Zack would always get the hottest girls in school while Screech would get nothing.

Watching this as a kid, I started to realize what women want. They want popular, good-looking guys with six-pack abs. And if you were smart or average-looking, you'd be stuck with an average, "not-so-cool" girl. There was even an episode where Zack stole the girl Screech was in love with since childhood—another great lesson that a good-looking, cool guy can swoop in and take your gal. Wasn't Zack awesome?

These were the lessons I had growing up as a kid. My own high school experience confirmed this reality, too. Attractive girls went for popular guys, and everyone else ate dust.

This is not real life. Television, the media, magazines, advertisements and high school aren't accurate pictures of the real world. The truth is what I talked about in Chapter 1: attraction is an emotional reaction and is triggered when a man displays his personality and masculine traits. In my early 20s, I tested this out, and it was 100 percent true. I worked on building out my personality and using tension, entertainment, and dominance, and it landed me dates and sex with amazing and beautiful women. I should note that I have very average looks and I'm not rich. When I started to teach clients these same principles, they got the same results. Your personality, aka your inner qualities, go a long way when it comes to meeting and attracting women.

But what about your outer qualities? What role does looks, money, and lifestyle play in the attraction game? Are they important?

As I've already said, the media has blown it up to make you think that your outer qualities are all that matter in attraction. They're not. However, they do help, and it's important to maximize all the different areas that make up your outer qualities. That's why I want to go over those areas and give you my very best practical tips to work with what you've got.

I call it the *four-step attraction amplifier*: health, wealth, appearance, and lifestyle. When you have your inner qualities on point and your outer qualities maximized, you'll be a machine at meeting and seducing women. There's one very important thing to remember when it comes to the four-step attraction amplifier:

> **You're working on your looks, money, lifestyle, and wealth for YOU, not for HER.**

The second you start working on these to attract a woman, you're back to playing the sucker's game that every other guy is playing: competing for women by making money or getting a six pack. You're wasting your time because (a) you're up against an enormous number of guys who already have the six pack and a seven-figure bank account and (b) because you now understand that your personality has a larger effect on a woman's interest in you. I've seen good-looking millionaires who can't hold a conversation, so they have to rely on prostitutes for any kind of intimacy.

Instead, I want you to work on these areas of your life so you become the optimal and most magnetic version of yourself possible. The benefit is a more fulfilling life, and one of the by-products is attracting more women.

However, health, wealth, lifestyle, and appearance don't necessarily "attract" women in the way you think they do. Instead, they offer some unique bonuses that help with dating in ways you've never thought. I'll go over them one by one, but first, you need to understand that maximizing your outer qualities is *not* an overnight fix. And it doesn't have to be. It's something you work on in the *background* while you concentrate more on your inner qualities. Your outer qualities are a work in progress, and the sooner you get started, the faster you'll get those areas of your life handled. My point is, I don't want you to get overwhelmed by the following information. It's impossible to optimize these in less than a year, but I urge you to still work on them so they work for you. Let's dig in.

***Quick note:** You may question how I know the following information, especially since I'm not citing any sources. Understand that I've read many books and articles, been to seminars, and even got coaching in the following areas. What lies ahead is all that knowledge crammed into specific and tangible steps I've seen work time and time again. Experiment with the below and see what works for you.*

OPTIMIZING YOUR HEALTH

Besides the obvious benefit of living longer, optimizing your health is great for balancing your emotions. Lifting weights, running, and eating nutritious foods assist in regulating your stress levels. When you regulate your stress levels, you can function better. You decrease your anxiety, feel happier, and have sustained energy.

Wouldn't it be great if you could meet women by feeling this way? People who don't get enough exercise and nutrition don't realize they're making day-to-day tasks harder on themselves. Eating properly and getting your blood pumping keeps your mind and body sharp. And naturally, if you focus on physical health, then you'll have a more toned and chiseled body, which does help women find you more physically attractive. Lots of wins here.

What's most important is feeling good. Don't just go to the gym because some magazine said that a woman's favorite body parts are your biceps and abs. Do women like biceps and abs? Some do, sure. But it won't determine if she's interested in you. It's a bonus.

What's the quickest way to incorporate this into your lifestyle? To sum it up in a few words, move heavy things and eat more nutrients. If you only focus on those two things in the health department, then you'll see some massive results, including weight loss and stable emotional health. Here's a few tips:

- Go to the gym three times per week for 45 minutes. I wouldn't even worry about an exercise plan for at least a month. Just get consistent with your schedule and build the habit of showing up at the gym. Run on the treadmill. Pick up some dumbbells. Do some push-ups. Focus on different body parts. After you've developed a habit, look into some programs such as *Starting Strength*, which can help you build a strong, muscular physique.

- Drink more water. The general rule is to drink eight 8 oz glasses of water known as the 8x8 rule. Water will keep you hydrated which helps with energy, focus, flushes toxins and keeps you from getting sick.

- Eat more greens. Adding more leafy green vegetables is going to add a lot more nutrition into your diet. Try to incorporate a salad with kale, arugula, and spinach with your meals. As time goes on, try eating a salad at least once a day. Another easy way to get greens into your diet is by drinking a green smoothie. I recommend a drink called the Green Monster (it's delicious).

- Get a powerful blender such as a Vitamix and make this drink every morning:
    - handful of leafy greens
    - 1 frozen banana
    - 1 cup of pineapple juice
    - 1 scoop of green powder

- Get your bloodwork done. Go to a doctor and get your blood checked to see if you have any nutritional or hormonal deficiencies. You could be low in certain nutrients or testosterone, which can cause low sex drive, mood swings, or general malaise.

This may seem like a lot right now, and it could overwhelm you to the point where you don't do anything. For now, pick one of these three areas and work on it in the background of your life. Join a gym or buy a blender or add salad ingredients to your grocery list. Pick one and run with it, and once you have that handled, move on to the next. The 88-year-old you will be thankful you did.

OPTIMIZING YOUR WEALTH

Optimizing your wealth is important because it gives you access and freedom. With more money, you can travel around the world, experience new hobbies, and have more time to do the things you want to do. These new experiences and adventures will also give you access to more women. With access to these new resources, you'll meet all types of women you might not otherwise meet. You'll also meet more women if you're making new friends who have similar hobbies and experiences.

Expert copywriter John Carlton said, "Money solves problems that not having money causes." This simple quote has given me a very healthy relationship with money, because it confirms that money *can* solve a lot of problems. You can absolutely buy happiness, but happiness might not be in the form of a Lamborghini or Rolex. Instead, it gives you access to personal trainers for proper strength training, a top-notch psychologist to work out emotional issues, healthier foods, or opportunities to donate to charitable causes. Don't think that more money equals more fancy stuff to impress people, because that's a game you can never win. Money means an *easier* route to a higher well-being. And of course, you can always treat yourself to nice items or experiences you enjoy.

I have some good news for you. Income does not always correlate to wealth. I know some people who make 30–40,000 dollars per year and have enough savings and investments to retire early. I also know people making 150,000 dollars per year who are in serious debt and living paycheck to paycheck. There's a lot of different ways to treat your money, but I want to give you some principles proven to help your finances, whether you're broke or already wealthy.

- Focus on income. What can you do to make more money? Can you get a raise at your work or get promoted? Is there a side hustle you can work on to make a few hundred or a few thousand extra dollars per month? Do you have an expertise in an area where you can do consulting or coaching? Do you have a business idea? Right now, with the way technology is moving, you can build a website within a week and start selling a product or service instantly. If you have an idea, get started on it right away and think "progress over perfection" so you get it done fast.

- Get rid of credit card debt. If you're in heavy debt, then I recommend you focus on this *before* you start saving. Your debt is costing you more money because every month you get charged finance fees. Make a plan to put any extra income toward alleviating your debt so you can wipe it out. Then start saving and investing. Debt is holding you back.

- Save 5–20 percent of your paycheck. Depending on your financial situation, it's always smart to save part of your paycheck. The money will come in handy when you have an emergency situation or want to put a down payment on a home, go on a big trip, or buy a new car. Saving will prevent you from going into future debt and can help build wealth for your future. Even if it's 50 dollars per month, get into the habit of saving so you can continue doing it over time. The bottom line here is to save more than you spend.

- Invest 5–20 percent of your paycheck. Money can work for you by investing in the proper areas. Your investments will make you more money over time and build wealth for your future and retirement.

Max out your 401K at work, especially if they match you. Start putting money into a Roth IRA since it's tax-free when you withdraw the funds at retirement. Add funds to a brokerage account and invest in less risky stocks known as ETFs/mutual funds (famous investor Warren Buffet says this is the best way to invest your money instead of just buying a few single stocks and crossing your fingers). You can also invest in yourself by funding your own side hustle or business. Whatever it is you decide to invest in, make it a habit to put some money toward an investment vehicle every month, even if it's 50 dollars. The future you will be happy you did.

- Invest in yourself. If you're reading this, then you've already done this by purchasing this book. Every month, set aside a little money for learning and growing. Get a new book. Get coaching in an area that will help you have a more fulfilling life (i.e., dating/relationships, wealth, health, appearance, and lifestyle). The more you grow and become a well-rounded person, the happier you'll become.

Note to the guys in high school and college: your best bet is to find a skill that's practical in the real world. That way you can easily create a side hustle, quickly get a job, or even create your own business. Find something you can learn now and for free on the Internet that will be useful to companies or the world in general. It wouldn't be the worst idea to find a skill related to sales or something in tech. Those are two industries that will never die. Some examples are cold-calling, website development, graphic design, software development, marketing management, etc. Mark Zuckerberg created Facebook when he was still in college, so there's no limit to what's possible.

I am not a financial advisor. These are some helpful tips I've learned as I studied personal finance. I recommend getting some books on this topic if you want to learn more and hiring a financial advisor to help with your finances.

Woah, there's a lot there! Now what? In this case, work from the top down. Start with a way to increase your income, then move on to debt and so on. Realistically, if you took two or three days, you could knock all this out because it's all systematic. Get real with the amount of money you make and the amount of money you owe and create a budget that allows you to save more than you spend.

OPTIMIZING YOUR APPEARANCE

Short, tall, fat, skinny, hunched over, facial scars, balding, wheelchair. I don't care what you look like or what's happened to your body or face over the years: fashion and grooming can increase your physical attractiveness. It's amazing how some simple tweaks can make you appear that much better.

I'm going to give you some universal and timeless techniques to optimize your outer appearance. What you won't read is any trendy advice that won't work 10 years down the road. If you want to look good, just follow this advice and you'll be on your way.

But first, why optimize our appearance? You're probably thinking, "Duh, to look sexy so women are attracted to me!" Yes, this definitely plays a role. More importantly, it does two things:

1. It buys you a few minutes after the hello.
2. It creates superficial confidence.

Let's go the extreme route for a second. Imagine a dirty, smelly, homeless person comes up to you and starts a conversation. How quickly will you dismiss him? Very. On the other hand, how willing are you to talk to a woman who's dressed to the nines, wearing amazing perfume, and looks like she just walked off a movie set? Very. The same goes with women. If you're wearing nicer clothes and are well groomed, it's easier for a woman to take you seriously. And can you blame her? When you're dressed properly and appear clean, you'll look like you have your act together.

Sometimes, dressing well is enough for a woman to decide within the first three minutes to sleep with you. But be very careful here. All I'm saying is that it can get you in the door. If you still fail to display your masculine qualities and practice the principles of attraction, it doesn't matter how nice you look; you won't trigger the emotional part of her brain.

Next, dressing well creates superficial confidence. When you look your best, you're going to *feel* your best. When I'm fresh out of the shower and getting dressed, I feel more ready for the day. When I'm in a proper suit and tie, I feel more powerful. Clothes can have that effect on you. I want to show you the right clothes to wear that'll give you a boost when you're with women, with friends, or at work.

- **Wear fitted clothes.** Your clothes should fit your body type. They shouldn't be skin-tight, just fitted. The shape of your body is attractive to women. When you're wearing baggy clothing, it doesn't give the same effect as when she can see your outline. All throughout fashion history, fitted has never gone out of style, and there's a reason for that; it looks good. Everything from your sweatpants to your suit and from your T-shirts to your button-downs should be fitted. Get a few pairs of pants, T-shirts, and button-downs and get them tailored to your body.

- **Get a suit.** Every man needs a nicely tailored suit. You can wear this for many occasions, and it looks very attractive. Ideally, you spend at least 1,000 dollars on a nice suit because it will look amazing and last you at least five or ten years. If you can't afford that, then spend as much as you can and wear the hell out of it.

- **Colors.** Make this easy on yourself. Don't worry about patterns or textures. Just get pants and shirts in black, white, gray, and navy blue. This is a great base to start with because those colors are always in style and always look good on men.

- **Get a stylist.** Make an appointment with a fashion stylist or fashion coach (you can email me at tripp@trippadvice.com for any recommendations) and schedule a few sessions to get your wardrobe in order. This is a one-time investment that goes a long way. Get a few of the right pieces of clothing and you'll never have to worry about it again. Stylists can also help you with a few pairs of proper shoes.

- **Shave your face.** The options are endless with facial hair. Your best bet is to be clean shaven or at most have a five o'clock shadow. Any more than that and you risk having a scraggly-looking beard that isn't groomed properly. Also, facial hair makes you look older, and it's better to skew young than old. And if you have a unibrow or unkempt eyebrows, get them tweezed and shaped.

- **Get a haircut.** If you're bald or balding, keep your hair short and tight. Longer hair with patches of bald is not attractive. On the other hand, shaved heads look just fine. If you're not lacking in the hair department, then go to a stylist and spend a minimum of 50 dollars. Get their opinion on the best haircut for your face shape, because it's different for everyone.

- **Glasses.** If you have glasses, get contacts. Otherwise, you risk wearing glasses that don't optimize your facial appearance. If you absolutely can't wear contacts, then go to any optical store and get a stylish pair.

- **Dental hygiene.** Brush your teeth twice a day. Floss twice a day. Scrape your tongue twice a day. Chew gum or mints before talking to any women.

- **Get cologne**. Search "top-rated cologne." Read a couple of articles and pick one. As much as I'd love to give you a suggestion, this book will be around for a long time, and I don't want to mention any brands that could be discontinued. There are a bunch of different types of cologne to consider: daytime colognes, beach colognes, club colognes, and the list goes on. Pick the best overall cologne and spray it on your wrists, front and back of neck, chest, and stomach before you go out. Cologne wears off, and you want to make sure she can smell you. Otherwise, what's the point?

Once again, there's lots here. Make a list and start knocking these out one at a time. No big rush. This doesn't have to be done overnight. Just continue ticking away at it as life moves on. Most importantly, don't forget about talking to women. Remember, inner qualities go further than outer qualities. A man with a serious lack of fashion can easily pick up a girl if he knows how to display his masculine qualities. Your style and grooming are just cherries on top that make it a little easier after the initial hello.

OPTIMIZING YOUR LIFESTYLE

I see lifestyle as how you spend your time. What are you doing on a day-to-day basis? Who are you spending time with? What activities are you doing? How much time do you spend with the people who care about you?

The areas of lifestyle to focus on are the people you spend time around, where you live, and the hobbies you take part in. Consider these the areas that are outside of your general line of work. This helps you attract more women for various reasons.

First, the people you surround yourself with can give you access to new experiences and new people. If you're mingling with the right person, you could, for example, get tickets to a baseball game in your city. At the hot dog stand, you might meet an amazing woman, or a friend might invite you to their birthday party, where you make more new friends and meet another hot girl.

Also, making friends can be good for your emotional support. Quality male friends can be a sounding board for your issues or general venting. Friendship is about making you a better person while also having a good time.

Second, where you live has a big effect on your mental health and the type of network you create. If you live in a city that is cold year-round and has a small population, it might be harder for you to meet a lot of women than if you lived in a big city with millions of people. Also, if you choose to live in a city that is big in an industry you're not part of, that could affect the types of close relationships you have and make it harder to connect. Furthermore, if you live in a place that has little sun and you're forced to live in small apartment, you might feel more depressed. As you can see, your location has a big effect on you.

Third, your activities and hobbies make your life more enjoyable, make you an interesting person, and give you the chance to meet all types of people. I strongly suggest never focusing solely on your work because it can mentally drain you and keep you in a box your whole life. We weren't meant to just eat, sleep, work, and die. I hope we can both agree that your life is more important than that.

- **Move to a big city.** The bigger the city, the better. I once had a client who lived in a town so small he practically knew everyone. Meeting women and making friends was extremely difficult for him. He wasn't ready to move quite yet, so his best option was to drive 30 minutes to the nearest bigger town and practice approaching women. To make your dating life and networking life easier, see if you can move to or close to a city of at least

500,000 people. You will have a larger pool of both women and potential friends to choose from.

- **Make friends who have similar interests.** After college, many men struggle to make new friends. One of the best ways to do this is to use your interests and hobbies as an outlet to meet new people. It doesn't get any easier than that because you already have a common interest! This could be rock-climbing, hiking, sailing, video gaming, live music, entrepreneurship, and more.

- **Make travel a priority.** Now that you know to start saving money, it's a good idea to create a goal for travel. From my experience, traveling is one of the best ways to spend your time. It's fun, it makes you more interesting, you learn about new cultures, and you challenge yourself by being in a new environment. The benefits are endless. You also get to meet new and different types of women. A solo trip somewhere across the world will be very beneficial to your overall lifestyle.

- **Get hobbies.** Like I said, life is short and should be filled with more than just eating, sleeping, and working. If you don't have any hobbies yet, then it's time to experiment. A good way to do this is to try one new hobby every month and see what sticks. Search "list of hobbies" and you'll get a load of ideas. My advice is to start with salsa dancing. It's practical, you can meet women, and it helps build confidence because you're learning a skill.

Start from the top down and make your way through this list. Again, it can be overwhelming, but work on one thing at a time and make small steps as you continue.

THE EYE CONTACT SECRET THAT ATTRACTS WOMEN

That said, how can you actually get a woman to come and approach you? First off, working on all these areas of your life will build a lot of self-esteem. Creating goals and putting together a healthy life is crucial to the way you feel about yourself. When you slowly tick away at the four-step attraction amplifier, you'll walk around feeling deserving of a beautiful woman. Your life is awesome, so why *wouldn't* she want to be part of it? Women can smell this confidence and self-assurance a mile away.

Of course, we can't just have you walking around and hoping for the best, so I want to teach you an eye contact secret that gets her approaching you. When you're out at a bar or social event, scan the room for eye contact. When you make eye contact with a girl, do *not* look away. Ninety-nine percent of the time, she'll be the first to look away. You must win this contest. If she holds it with you for two or three seconds, flash a smile. Whether she smiles or not, go up and talk to her. Use the line "Hi, I saw you over here and you look nice." I've mentioned this line earlier and works for any situation, including this one.

This is a trick I call "forcing eye contact." Just be sure to scan the room and not deliberately stare at a girl for too long. Otherwise, it can come off as creepy. Also, understand that you can use this any time you want. I need to reiterate that nothing should hold you back from going out and meeting women. The four-step attraction amplifier is and will always be part of your life, so you don't need to wait for any accomplishments in these areas for you to start meeting women. The best time to start talking to women is right now.

WHERE TO MEET HIGH-QUALITY WOMEN IN PERSON

Women are everywhere. They're all around you. But you need the best plan of action for where to meet them. The absolute best place to meet women is where they congregate in your town. Lots of guys judge certain areas like bars or clubs just because of the environment. I want you to look at these hyper-social scenes as nothing but a place where women hang out. And that's where you want to be if you want to get good at attracting women. The more women you can approach in a given year, the better you'll be.

Below is a list of different places to meet women, so you can't complain that there aren't any women in your town. If you still feel that way after reading the list below, I recommend you drive to the next closest city to find more women.

Bars and Clubs
This is the number one spot to practice approaching and meeting single women. The reality is, lots of single women go out, so there's a ton of women to talk to at bars or clubs. Find the hottest spots in your city and try going there on the weekend. These places can be quite intimidating because the music is loud and it's crowded, but if you can master approaching here, you'll be in great shape for any other location.

Public Places
This is good for when you're out during the day. They include the

sidewalk, malls, grocery stores, shops, outdoor malls, the beach, parks, etc. When the weather's nice, you'll find an endless number of women to talk to. I highly recommend making it a habit to visit these places when you start this journey of talking to women.

Meetup.com

This is a great site to find events in your city. You can search by distance, topic, and date. It has events for singles, hobbies, business, socializing, gaming, and more. Go to events that interest you or pick some you just want to try out.

Events on Social Media

Depending on what's popular when you're reading this book, you can always find an "events" section. Similar to Meetup.com, Facebook lists events happening in your area and organizes them by day of the week. There's usually a lot to choose from and they can include anything from concerts and festivals to art events. Attend these! Go alone and start chatting up people around you.*

Singles Events

You can find these by Googling "singles events [city]". Sometimes, it's speed-dating or just a party with all single people. Buy a ticket and check these out. It's a great place to practice displaying your inner qualities with people you know are single.

Networking Events

Depending on what industry you work in, there's always an option for a networking event. It's a very common place to meet someone because of how many men and women attend. There's also local and national networking groups. Search Google and see what you can find. Go to these and practice your social skills.

The Gym and Exercise Classes

Of course, there are always beautiful women at the gym. Over the years, lots of guys have asked me how best to meet women at the gym. Your best bet is to spark up a conversation when she's *not* in the middle of her workout. Catch her at the end, when it gives you more time to talk to her without interruption. Also, join workout classes like meditation, yoga, spin, or Pilates. Lots of women attend these, and you can start conversations with them after class. A good opener is "Hey, I'm [name]. What did you think of the class?"

Going out with friends versus going out solo. If you're going out to meet women, I highly recommend you either go alone or with friends who are also interested in meeting women. If you ever go out with friends to just go shopping or have a few drinks at the bars, it's rare they'll be as proactive as you when talking to women, which will then hold you back. One of the best things you can do, albeit the most challenging, is going out alone. I can't recommend this enough. In theory, you don't need wingmen to help you meet women. It's always going to be up to you to attract a woman and either bounce her or get her number. Rarely have I ever had women ask me where my friends are; they assume they're around the club or bar. When you go out alone, you really hone in on the skill of meeting women in any circumstance because it teaches you how to act without relying on anyone.

5 BIGGEST MISTAKES GUYS MAKE IN ONLINE DATING AND WHAT TO DO ABOUT THEM

While this book mostly discusses how to meet and seduce women in person, I realize that online dating will inevitably be part of your repertoire—as it should! Online dating is a great way to meet women. Just don't solely rely on it, or you'll never be able to hone the skill of attracting a woman in person. No matter what, you'll need this skill, because if you meet a woman online, you'll eventually have to get her on a date.

MISTAKE #1:
Messaging for Too Long Without Getting a Phone Number

Remember dominance? This is the concept of moving the interaction forward. You don't need to message a woman back and forth multiple times to get her number. If she's responsive and you've each messaged four to six times, then you're ready to get her number to move it to a date. You can say, "You seem cool. Let's text and grab a glass of wine sometime. Here's my number. What's yours?"

MISTAKE #2:
Terrible Photos

The options are endless with what kind of photos to put on your dating profile. It's best to stick with the basics to best optimize your appearance. Don't put up blurry photos, multiple photos of you and your friends, or photos of you with your shirt off. Instead, put up photos that clearly show you, your face, and your body. Put up one of you and friends and a few of you doing activities you enjoy. She needs to see you and have something to comment on. I suggest hiring a professional photographer to get these done. That way, you can use a few professional photos that make you look your best.

MISTAKE #3:
Lame Opening Messages

Don't get lazy here. This is your chance to get her to respond. You'll rarely get a response if you say "Hey, how are you?" or "Hey" or "What's up?" or "How's your day?" Don't make her do all the work. Make it easy for her to respond by commenting on something in one of her pictures or on her bio. Here's where you have to get creative. Don't call out something that's extremely obvious because every other guy is doing the same thing. Try and pick something unique in a picture, like something from the background, or bring up a something from her bio that you can actually talk about. For example, if she plays piano and you do, too, you'll be able to have a real discussion about that, so mention it! No matter what, never *ever* say something about her looks, because she's hearing that 10 times per day.

MISTAKE #4:
Not Sending a Second Message

I never condone chasing a girl or being too needy, but this is where you should try a second time. If after the first message she doesn't message you back for three or more days, then send her a second message. This is a bit of a number's game, but it can work to your benefit. Some women get hundreds of messages per day, so she might finally see you if you send a second message. You can either say something completely new and different or jokingly use this: "You don't write. You don't call. We used to be so good together :D" Try that out for women you're really interested in, and a few should respond.

MISTAKE #5:
Spending Too Much Time Online

Online dating can get addicting, and if you have a good profile, you could potentially get a lot of matches and be messaging many women. While this is a good thing, it can also hinder your most important skill: meeting women in person. If you're swiping right on a lot of women, focus on getting a few on a date. Only use one or two apps and one site so you don't bog yourself down with too much messaging. Don't waste too much time online. The most important thing to do is meet and seduce women in person, not over messaging.

HOW TO BECOME INSTANTLY CONFIDENT

How does all this relate to confidence? Well, it's almost impossible to sit at home, do nothing, and meditate yourself to confidence. If you know of anyone who's done that, please send them my way so I can pay them to teach me.

We've been using confidence as a noun, like it's a thing you have. However, I've found that confidence is not something you have; it's something you do. You gain confidence by taking action. To gain confidence, you need to *do* confidence. Here's a formula to help with that:

Confidence = Competence + The Ability to Step into the Unknown

Competence is the ability to do something successfully, and the way you become competent in something is with deliberate practice. If you want to feel comfortable talking to girls, you have to practice over and over.

When I was 24, I dedicated two years of my life to approaching women and learning how to handle rejection. I was going out four to seven times per week, and twice I did 21 days in a row. I practiced talking to women, flirting with women, getting physical with women, and beating my fear. You don't have to do it that much. I went overboard, which is probably why I'm now teaching this to men like you. But it's important to treat this seriously if you want solid results. Everything takes practice.

When I say "deliberate practice," I mean really giving it your best shot and being disciplined. For example, every chapter in this book has action steps. Follow them and give it your all. Complete the exercises. Finish this book and then do the exercises again. If you do that, I promise you'll feel way more competent with attracting women. Some guys feel a little weird about treating dating as "practice," but there's an actual skill set to it. When you learn how to communicate with the opposite sex and *do* confidence, it makes a world of difference.

The ability to step into the unknown (i.e., step outside your comfort zone) is another part in the confidence formula and plays a big part in this. The best way to do this is through a process of *systematic desensitization*. That's a five-dollar word for using baby steps to make yourself feel competent in something. For example, systematic desensitization is a process used for things like fear of spiders. Using baby steps, overcoming your fear would look something like this:

Step 1: Think of a spider
Step 2: Look at a photo of a spider
Step 3: Look at a real spider in a closed box
Step 4: Hold the box containing the spider
Step 5: Let a spider crawl on your desk
Step 6: Let a spider crawl on your shoe
Step 7: Let a spider crawl on your sleeve
Step 8: Let a spider crawl on your bare arm

As you can see, this baby-step process takes it a little further and further each time. The person feels more comfortable with the unknown as they move the needle further and further. You can do the same thing with talking to beautiful women:

Step 1: Think about a cute girl
Step 2: Look at a photo of a cute girl
Step 3: Walk by a cute girl in real life
Step 4: Wave at a cute girl

Step 5: Ask a cute girl for directions
Step 6: Tell a cute girl she's cute and walk away
Step 7: Start a conversation with a cute girl
Step 8: Continue a conversation with a cute girl

You keep baby stepping up and up the ladder until you get more and more comfortable.

Here's another secret most people don't know. The more you practice stepping into the unknown, the less you'll have to fear in this world. Practicing doing scary things helps make you stronger. Consistently pushing yourself out of your comfort zone prevents you from being afraid of things, even if they're things you haven't done yet! For example, if you decided one month to go skydiving, the next month to hold a snake, the next month to give a speech in front of strangers, and the next month to hike a tall mountain, then you'd be getting yourself used to doing scary things. The next month's activity might not be as bad because you know how to tackle your fear.

Now is your chance to do that by using the information in this book. Once I conquered my fear of talking to women, I found that it translated into multiple areas of my life. Talking to all strangers got easier, conversing in front a crowd got easier, and having difficult conversations with people got easier. So this is a good start for you, since you're going to talk to a lot of girls in the next few weeks.

CONQUERING APPROACH ANXIETY

One of the biggest things that'll hold you back from getting results with women and dating is approach anxiety. Lots of guys won't even attempt to approach a woman because they're too afraid. If anyone understands that, it's me. In fact, I still have approach anxiety. It's not as debilitating as it was 10 years ago, but it still exists. And the truth is, it'll never go away. It only gets smaller and smaller, which then makes it easier and easier to deal with.

Don't feel bad about being afraid to approach women. It's completely normal. Most men will never approach a woman in their entire life while sober. It's their loss, not ours. So how do we deal with this?

First, you need to understand right off the bat that rejection will happen. It's inevitable, and it's part of getting better. If I'm using the guitar-playing analogy, it's synonymous with trying to play a song on the guitar. If I told you to learn how to play the guitar and never make a mistake, you'd laugh at me. Of course you'll make mistakes!

The good news is, rejection really isn't that bad. Now you might not know that yet, because you haven't put yourself out there to get rejected, but take my word for it since I've been rejected hundreds of times: the worst that can happen is her walking away. That's it. It's your turn to experience it for yourself, so laugh and realize how much it doesn't matter.

The only true way to beat approach anxiety is to approach. The best way for you to conquer your approach anxiety is to make it a mass numbers game. Don't let anyone tell you differently. This is the most effective way. But you don't have to flirt with every girl you see. You can just spark up friendly conversation or even ask for directions. Take baby steps.

Earlier, I mentioned a process called systematic desensitization, which involves taking baby steps to desensitize you to something scary. It's an effective tool for overcoming approach anxiety. Here's a good guideline to follow when you're first starting this process:

Step 1: Think about a cute girl
Step 2: Look at a photo of a cute girl
Step 3: Walk by a cute girl in real life
Step 4: Wave at a cute girl
Step 5: Ask a cute girl for directions
Step 6: Tell a cute girl she's cute and walk away
Step 7: Start a conversation with a cute girl
Step 8: Continue a conversation with a cute girl

Continue repeating that process until you get comfortable with Step 8. Then rinse and repeat.

Another reason men are scared to approach a woman is because they don't know what to say. We're going to dive further into this topic in Chapter 3, but for now, arm yourself with a few openers to use for Step 8 so you don't freeze up when you see a girl you want to talk to:

"Hi, I saw you over here and you look nice."

This opener works like magic at a party, bar, club, grocery store, or event. It even works on the sidewalk. You can use it literally anywhere. Next, arm yourself with a conversation continuer. Here's a good one:

"Are you from [city you're in]?" Then continue to talk about how much you either like or dislike the city.

That's it. Women rarely remember the opener, so if you can jump to another topic very quickly and get her engaged, then you'll be good to go.

Another thing to remember is that women want to meet you. Guys believe women are just ready to reject us at any moment. The only reason why any man thinks that is because he doesn't value himself and has low self-esteem. But that's all nonsense chatter in your head. Single women are looking for single men. They expect to be approached and want to give guys a shot. Now, of course, some are shy or are having a bad day or not in the mood to talk, and those are the ones that'll reject you. But let's not let a couple sour apples get in the way of you meeting an amazing woman.

ACTION STEPS:

Sign up for a gym and plan to go three times per week for 45 minutes.

Take five percent of your next paycheck and put it in a savings account.

Go to a barber/stylist and ask for haircut that fits well with your face shape.

Sign up for a salsa dancing class, and if that doesn't exist in your city, Google "list of hobbies" and pick one to do once a week.

Use systematic desensitization and do one round of Steps 1–8.

Remember, do these above action steps and continue to tick away at the four-step attraction amplifier in the background of your life. There's no rush—just make sure you continue moving forward with them.

Now, let's get into some techniques for becoming a master conversationalist so you can talk to any beautiful woman you come across. Head on over with me to Chapter 3.

— ∾ —

36 QUESTIONS THAT HACK A WOMAN'S MIND AND MAKE HER LOVE YOU (SCIENTIFICALLY PROVEN!)

You've learned about the inner qualities and outer qualities that trigger attraction in a woman. But how do you put this into practice? What are you supposed to say to a woman when you meet her? How do you continue a conversation when you run out of things to say?

In this chapter, I'll teach you the topics of conversation women love. You'll also learn the 36 questions that have been proven to help you connect with a woman more quickly. Finally, I'll show you an easy formula that makes conversation with any woman flow.

ATTRACTION VS. INVESTMENT

In Chapter 1, we went over the inner qualities that trigger a woman's attraction (tension, entertainment, and dominance). You build sexual tension, entertain yourself, and display dominance. However, this is not the whole puzzle. These are the overall principles, but you must also build *investment*.

When a woman is invested in you and the conversation, she'll want to keep seeing you or go on a date with you. Without investment, women become flaky by not responding to your texts. They won't give you their numbers. They just flat out won't be *that* interested.

So why isn't attraction enough to get a girl interested in you? Why does she have to be invested? Let's compare it to buying a car. Let's pretend you go to an Audi dealership because you've heard they have nice cars. You walk on the lot and you see lots of amazing cars. You're "attracted." A car salesman comes up to you and asks if you see anything interesting. You point to the Audi A4 and ask how much it is. Boom! It's even in your price range. The salesman then says, "Okay, we can get that to you right now. Just hand over the money and it's yours."

Now, wait a second. You're not ready to buy it quite *yet*. You want to test drive it. You want to sit inside it. You want to see if there's other colors. You want to see how it handles the road. You're not ready to buy it yet because you're not *invested*. The salesman jumped the gun. He needs to show you the ins and outs of the car to get you invested and ready to bite.

It's the same with meeting women. You want to trigger attraction and get her invested in you. Remember, women are not as quick to want to date and sleep with a guy. It takes more time for her to get to know you, see your masculine qualities, and become invested. The way you'll get a woman invested is simply by spending time with her. This is why you continue talking to a woman while simultaneously building tension, providing entertainment, and displaying dominance.

Let me teach you what to say to a girl and how to hold a conversation so you can build investment.

CHICK CRACK: THE TOPICS OF CONVERSATION THAT WOMEN LOVE

Don't forget to visit http://www.trippadvice.com/chick-crack/ and download a free video that explains all the topics!

In the previous chapters, I've given you a few openers to use when you meet a girl. Here's my favorite:

"Hi, I saw you over here and you look nice."

I want you to remember that the opener *does not* matter. It just gets you into conversation. Rarely will a woman ever remember how you approached her. She'll only remember her feelings of attraction and what happened after the opening line.

Astrology Signs

It's almost magic how many women love talking about their astrology signs. Even if they don't believe in signs, you can always move a conversation toward that. There's always an opinion on the topic. It can go something like this:

Me: Hi, I saw you over here and you look nice.

Her: Hi there.

Me: How are you doing today?

Her: I'm okay.

Me: Just okay? Let me guess: Mercury is in retrograde so you're kinda in the dumps.

Her: What does that mean?

Me: Wait, you don't know your sign? I'm an Aries.

Her: Oh yeah! I'm a Virgo.

Me: So what does that say about you?

Her: Well, I pay a lot of attention to detail and can be intimidating to men.

Me: Well, you're freaking me out right now, so I don't know how much longer I can be here. Haha. So what do you know about Aries?

Her: Well, you guys are patient, loyal, and hard-working.

Me: Why thank you.

That's just a sample of how a conversation can go when you're getting into zodiac signs. Here's what it might look like if she doesn't have any interest:

Me: Hey, I'm Tripp. I haven't met you yet.

Her: Hi there.

Me: How are you doing today?

Her: I'm okay.

Me: Just okay? Let me guess: Mercury is in retrograde so you're kinda in the dumps.

Her: What does that mean?

Me: Wait, you don't know your sign? I'm an Aries.

Her: That stuff isn't real, just a bunch of nonsense.

Me: Really? I think it's quite interesting. Are your friends really into that stuff?

Her: Yeah, they talk about it sometimes.

Me: What do you believe in? Ghosts?

Her: Well, maybe. The verdict is out on that one.

Me: I thought my house was haunted when I was a kid. It would make weird sounds at night and it freaked me out.

Her: Yeah, me too!

Now, of course, not every conversation goes as smoothly as that, but you can see that this topic can go in either direction and still result in a conversation. Research has shown that a large percentage of women do believe in astrology because they believe more in the supernatural than men do. Try bringing this up in conversation and you'll see how well it gets things going.

People-Watching and Assumptions

If you approach a woman and you're around people, you can use them for a topic of conversation. This can be a topic you bring up in the middle of the conversation and not so much right off the bat. Imagine that you're talking to her and a man in a suit walks by. You could say something like this:

"Wow, he looks like he's going somewhere important. What do you think he does for a living? Lawyer?"

Or a woman wearing a brightly colored skirt walks by and you say this:

"That's an interesting look. Would you ever wear that?"

Or maybe you're at a bar and you see a couple sitting together:

"Alright, look at these two. What do you think? First date? Married? Colleagues?"

Commenting on other people makes a fun game and creates what I call a "we bubble" because you're acting as if you're on the same team. In a sense, it's you two versus everyone else. Steal some of these examples and even come up with your own. Conversation is about accessing your creative side. The more you approach and practice, the easier it will become.

Hypothetical Situations

These make any conversation fun, especially if you're talking to a group of people. The best part is, there doesn't have to be any segue. Just bring them up any time you want. Here are some examples:

"Would you ever marry someone your parents wouldn't approve of?"

"What if you had the superpower of invisibility? How would you use it?"

"What if you were dating someone and you found out he was homeless?"

Use those hypothetical questions if conversation with a woman starts to die out. These work well because they make conversation interesting. People love to answer questions about their opinions, so it's rare for a woman to decline the question. Get creative and see if you can come up with some on your own. Otherwise, use the above examples.

Questions Regarding Male and Female Dynamics

Do you want to know one of the many reasons why the magazine *Cosmopolitan* sells so well? It's because the front cover is filled with headlines regarding dating, sex, and relationships. Women love talking about this stuff. Ninety-nine percent of the time, if you bring up something related to male and female dynamics, a woman will be eager to chime in. It makes for an interesting and flowing conversation.

Here are some examples to bring up when talking to her:

"Do you think women like sex more than men?"

"Do you think it's weird to go on a date with someone more than three times in a week if you've just met?"

"Should women pay for a guy on the first date?"

"Do you think chivalry is dead? Do women still like it?"

In general, people love sharing their opinions and they love being heard. Combine that with a topic women love, and you'll see how well it gets the conversation going.

How do you use all these topics in conversation? You have a few options. You can either use them to get conversation flowing or you can put them in your back pocket for when you truly run out of things to say. The choice is yours. Here's a sample of what a conversation in a bar or a social setting might look like:

Note: The text in square brackets explains how I'm displaying inner qualities during conversation.

Me: Hi, I saw you over here and you look nice.

Her: Hey.

Me: Someone told me earlier today that astrology signs are made-up lies. What do you think?

Her: Is this a pick-up line?

Me: Yes. Now answer the question (smile) [dominance].

Her: I totally believe in it. I'm a Sagittarius.

Me: Let me guess. That means you get very upset when guys come up to you asking about signs [entertainment].

Her: Haha! No, Sagittarius means I'm really extroverted and outgoing.

Me: I can tell (smile)! Okay, what's an Aries like? That's my sign.

Her: Hmm… I'm not sure

Me: Look real quick at that guy walking by. He's wearing pink pants. Would you be embarrassed if your boyfriend walked around in those pants [people watching]?

Her: I don't have a boyfriend, and no, probably not.

Me: You should have a boyfriend. It's all the rage these days. You get dinners and stuff and, if you're lucky, maybe even a hot make-out session in the back of a convertible [entertainment].

Her: I should only be so lucky!

Me: Let me ask you something. Do you think chivalry is dead [male/female dynamics]?

Her: I do! Nobody ever opens the door for me anymore. What's the deal with that?

Me: Aww, poor baby. Come here. You need a hug (go in for hug) [tension].

Her: That was a good hug (smile).

Me: I've been practicing for years. Tell me something interesting about you [tension].

Here, I tried to show you a tougher conversation in which the girl is not particularly receptive to you. That way, you can see how to best handle it. Notice how I interspersed all the inner qualities and the topics of conversation. To build tension, stand directly in front of her, make great eye contact, and speak in downward tonality. This would be a great start to conversation and could easily lead to a phone number or a drink back at your place.

I want to take this further. Let me teach you a formula to help make conversation flow even easier.

HOW TO NEVER RUN OUT OF THINGS TO SAY

When you're talking to a girl, it's easy to go totally blank and have nowhere to go in the conversation. That's the biggest fear for most guys. As you know, you can use the topics of conversation women love, and I'm also going to teach you my extraction formula so you don't have to solely rely on them.

Natural conversation is based on tangents. In every conversation, someone is asking a question, making a statement, or both. All you need to do is ask a question or make a statement when you're talking to a girl. That's it and nothing more.

Most guys take the easy way out and rapid fire a bunch of questions and let the women do all the work. This is a bad idea because you'll make it more difficult to get her invested. How can she become attracted or invested in a man who's just interviewing her? How will she see his personality and masculine traits? She won't. In order to get her more invested, you'll need to do most of the talking and use more statements than questions.

The easiest way to do this is to practice *active listening*, which means paying close attention to what she says. This is so you can extract a word from what she says and either make a statement or ask a follow-up question. This makes it easy to continue conversation when you're struggling with what to say next. For example, let's say you ask what her astrological sign is. She says she's a Virgo. Your keyword here is *Virgo*. Now you can either ask a question or make a statement regarding Virgo.

Here are some examples:

"What kind of traits does a Virgo have?" (question)
"I dated a Virgo once. That was an interesting experience." (statement)

Preferably, repeat the statement to get her invested and get her asking *you* a question. This way, she can get to know you. Let's use another example, this time not using one of the "chick crack" topics. The keyword here is *Detroit*.

Me: Are you from Chicago?
Her: No, I'm from Detroit.
Me: Detroit. I was there for a wedding last year. The place seems kind of empty. (statement)

Or

Me: Are you from Chicago?
Her: No, I'm from Detroit.
Me: Interesting. You didn't like it enough, so you came here? (question)

Or

Me: Are you from Chicago?
Her: Yup.
Me: Cool. What part? (question)
Her: Highland Park.
Me: Oh cool, I have friends from there. That's a nice area. (statement)

Or

Me: Are you from Chicago?
Her: Yup.
Me: Cool. What part? (question)
Her: Highland Park.

Me: Did you like growing up there? (question)

See all the different ways you could go with extracting just one word? To get the keyword when you're talking to a woman, you need to practice active listening. Otherwise, you can miss it. Another way to work on this is by creating *conversation cards.*

Take 10 index cards and write a different noun or verb on each one. By the end, on each of your 10 index cards you should have a different word such as "running" or "book." Go through each card and pretend the word is what you're extracting from a woman's sentence. Practice saying a statement and a question regarding each word. It can go something like this:

RUNNING
Q: When did you start getting into running?
S: I rarely ever run, but I like going on daily walks.

BOOK
Q: What's the best book you've read this year?
S: I'm reading *Magnetic* right now and I highly recommend it.

TIME
Q: Do you ever use a watch to tell the time? I always use my phone.
S: I feel there's never enough time in the day to get things done.

This exercise is endless. You can even create 50 index cards and roll through them whenever you want to practice continuing a conversation. If you combine this skill with having a few chick crack topics in your back pocket, you'll be a master at conversing. Now I want to add another layer of being able to ask powerful questions.

WHAT TO SAY WHEN YOU FLIRT WITH A GIRL

Flirting is what moves you from friend/acquaintance into potential lover. It is the way you're going to avoid the friend zone and make her sexually excited by you. Once you learn how to master flirting and add it into your conversation you're going to see a serious change in the way women interact with you.

Most men are too scared to flirt with women because they're afraid of getting rejected. When you avoid flirting you get thrown into the friend zone, because she won't be able to see you as a potential mate. You must remember that if you're not flirting, you're not creating Tension. Tension (T) is one of the crucial components of TED for building attraction. Understand that friends talk and lovers flirt.

Flirting is the subtle art of showing interest in a woman. I say subtle because flirting is not an overt action. The mystery behind flirting is what makes it attractive to a woman. I want to show you a technique that you can use for flirting called push/pull. This is where you will be metaphorically "pushing" her away and "pulling" her toward you with your words. Push/pull is great for showing subtle interest in a woman.

Pushing - When *pushing* you will be saying things that make you appear disinterested, however doing it jokingly. This way she will not take you serious and understand that you are flirting with her. One tip is to always smile when delivering these lines so it doesn't come off so serious. Here are some examples:

"You're an accountant? You must be such a nerd."

"I don't think this could work out between us, you're just not my type."

"That's it we're breaking up. This relationship is over."

"Let's find a guy for you tonight here at the bar. I know we can find someone amazing for you."

"Oh stop being such a brat!"

Although these examples are out of context, try and imagine when you might say these in conversation. The idea behind *pushing* is to show a playful disinterest. She will know you're joking when you smile but it will also show that you're not desperate to have her.

Pulling - To balance out *pushing* you want to incorporate *pulling* into your repertoire. If you're pushing too much it's going to get old, fast. You want to make sure she still feels some sort actual interest when you're with her. Here are some examples:

"Those dimples are so adorable."

"I'm not sure what it is yet but there's something I like about you."

"You have great style."

"Come closer I want to be able to hear you."

"I like that you're always laughing, your new nickname is Giggles."

Just like *pushing* you don't want to *pull* too much because then you'll be giving her too much interest. Balance the two out by using 1-2 push lines and a 1-2 pull lines in your interaction. You can use the ones I gave you above or come up with a few on your own to make it more natural.

5 WAYS TO TOUCH A GIRL TO MAKE HER WANT YOU

It's not absolutely necessary to do much touching before you first kiss. A kiss can happen without having ever touched her previously in the night. But, I wanted to give you a few pointers on how to break the touch barrier with a girl either on a date or before a date if you feel the desire to connect with her physically.

The High-Five: Use this only once in the night whether it's the first time you're meeting her or a first date (or both). When you give her a high-five don't just slap her hand but grab it gently and hold it for a second while giving her eye contact. Then let go and never do it again the rest of the night.

The Twirl: This is a great one to use when you're on a date. After you've had a drink/dinner and you're walking with her randomly take her hand and twirl her. It creates a nice playful vibe and connects you two on a physical level.

The Shoulder Touch: Use this once in a night. When she says something that's interesting or surprising, softly cup her shoulder with the mirroring hand. For example, if she says, "I'm from Dallas", grab her shoulder gently for 2-3 seconds and say "No way, you don't seem like you'd be from there." While this move isn't sexual in nature, it helps get her comfortable feeling touch from you.

The Hug: When you first meet a girl and you're talking give her a hug when she says something you like. And it can be anything.

For example if she says, "I'm from Dallas" you can say "No way I love people from Dallas!" and give her a hug. It seems ridiculous but it works well when you have a big smile on your face and you're in a social environment such as a bar.

The Stomach/Waist Touch: Have you ever touched a friend on the arm or shoulder when you feel fired up and you're making a point about something? Usually it's like a small poke or light touch. That's what I want you to do here but instead lightly use the back of your hand and touch her stomach or waist. For example if she says, "I'm from Dallas," you can say, "Oh nice, yeah I have actually always wanted to go there," and simultaneously touch her stomach or waist with the back of your fingers for 1-2 seconds.

HOW TO BE A MORE INTERESTING PERSON IN CONVERSATION

At this point in my life I find it fairly easy to talk to almost anyone about anything. This is a skill I've cultivated over the years. And if you learn how to do it you can have interesting conversation with anyone you meet. I want to share a formula I have to be able to do that:

Curiosity + Sharing = Interesting & Ongoing Conversation

Let's start with curiosity. Some people are naturally curious and others aren't. If you are then this process will be easier for you. If not, then I ask you to dig deep down inside and find your curious spark. Curiosity will help you learn more about what's going on in the world.

If you take the time to learn more about what's going on in the world such as keeping up with current events, reading fiction and non-fiction books, watching films, watching YouTube videos, going out to new restaurants, and experiencing events in your city then you'll broaden your conversation capabilities. Get curious and try some of these! Everything I just listed is something to bring up in conversation and talk about.

Next, you need to share these experiences and information with the women you talk to. Did you learn something interesting from a new book? Did something happen today in the news? Did you watch a weird YouTube video? Did you go to a cool new place in your city? Share this with the person you're talking to so you can prevent running out of things to say.

Also, it's important to note that the more you take the time to learn, read, watch and experience the easier it is to join conversations. Whenever someone brings up a topic you know about you can join in. And if you don't know what someone is talking about then learn from them! Ask them questions and soak up some new knowledge that you can bring to your next conversations.

Here's a sample schedule you could use to start taking in more knowledge and experiences:

Everyday read the news for 10 minutes.
Everyday watch one of the latest trending videos on YouTube.
Everyday go to the front page of Reddit.com and read 2-3 headlines.
Every week try going to one new place, restaurant, or event in your city.
Every month read one non-fiction book on any topic that peaks your interest
Every year travel to a new city or country for vacation.

Try this out and you'll start seeing your knowledge grow vastly. Don't forget to use this to open up and continue conversations with the people you're talking to.

36 QUESTIONS THAT MAKE HER LOVE YOU

In 1997 Arthur Aron, a psychologist at Stony Brook University, did an experiment to see if intimacy could be accelerated between two people if they were asked a specific set of questions. Each man and woman had to sit down, look into each other's eyes, and answer each question as honestly as possible. Dr. Aron concluded that the people in the study *did* feel a closeness to each other. These questions have been used to help strengthen relationships and marriages, and I've found they can help even when you meet someone for the first time (similar to the actual study).

When do you use these questions? I suggest using them after you've spent at least 15 minutes talking to a girl. The questions are quite personal, and it would be strange to ask them so soon in a conversation. Pick ones you'd be interested in answering yourself. She'll ask you the same question back, so you need an answer. You can even show her the study and answer the questions back and forth to each other on a second or third date. For now, I'm going to list the questions below and put an asterisk after the ones I think would be good to use in your initial interaction.

1. Given the choice of anyone in the world, whom would you want as a dinner guest?*

2. Would you like to be famous? In what way?*

3. Before making a telephone call, do you ever rehearse what you're going to say? Why?

4. What would constitute a "perfect" day for you?*

5. When did you last sing to yourself? To someone else?*

6. If you could live to the age of 90 and retain either the mind or body of a 30-year-old for the last 60 years of your life, which would you want?

7. Do you have a secret hunch about how you will die?

8. Name three things you and your partner appear to have in common.

9. For what in your life do you feel most grateful?*

10. If you could change anything about the way you were raised, what would it be?

11. Take four minutes and tell your partner your life story in as much detail as possible.

12. If you could wake up tomorrow having gained any one quality or ability, what would it be?*

13. If a crystal ball could tell you the truth about yourself, your life, the future, or anything else, what would you want to know?*

14. Is there something you've dreamed of doing for a long time? Why haven't you done it?*

15. What is the greatest accomplishment of your life?*

16. What do you value most in a friendship?

17. What is your most treasured memory?*

18. What is your most terrible memory?

19. If you knew that in one year you would die suddenly, would you change anything about the way you are now living? Why?

20. What does friendship mean to you?

21. What roles do love and affection play in your life?

22. Alternate sharing something you consider a positive characteristic of your partner. Share a total of five items.

23. How close and warm is your family? Do you feel your childhood was happier than most other people's?

24. How do you feel about your relationship with your mother?

25. Make three true "we" statements each. For instance, "We are both in this room feeling…"

26. Complete this sentence: "I wish I had someone with whom I could share…"

27. If you were going to become a close friend with your partner, please share what would be important for him or her to know.

28. Tell your partner what you like about them; be very honest this time and say things you might not say to someone you've just met.

29. Share with your partner an embarrassing moment in your life.

30. When did you last cry in front of another person? By yourself?*

31. Tell your partner something you like about them already.

32. What, if anything, is too serious to be joked about?

33. If you were to die this evening with no opportunity to communicate with anyone, what would you most regret not having told someone? Why haven't you told them yet?

34. Your house, containing everything you own, catches fire. After saving your loved ones and pets, you have time to safely make a final dash to save any one item. What would it be? Why?*

35. Of all the people in your family, whose death would you find most disturbing? Why?

36. Share a personal problem and ask your partner's advice on how he or she might handle it. Also, ask your partner to reflect back to you how you seem to be feeling about the problem you've chosen.

Try a few of these out when you're talking to a woman and see what comes of it. Like I said above, I put an asterisk after the ones I think would be most appropriate and interesting for a first-time interaction, but if you want to try some others, have at it!

ACTION STEPS:

• Get index cards and write a noun or verb on 10 cards to practice the extraction formula.

• Approach one girl and ask her about her astrology sign.

• Approach one girl and use a push and pull line to verbally flirt

---

• In one of the above approaches, ask one of the 36 questions.

If approaching girls is still hard for you I recommend going back to using the "Systematic Desensitization" method in Chapter 2.

Now that you've learned how to talk to girls and hold a conversation, it's going to be important to know how *she's* feeling when you're talking to her. Join me in the next chapter, where I'll tell you the secrets of learning if she likes you and how to escalate from there.

CHAPTER 4:

7 HIDDEN "BODY LANGUAGE CLUES" THAT SHE LIKES YOU

W hen I was first learning how to meet women, I always thought that being able to tell if she was attracted to you was a superpower. It was completely foreign to me. How can you read a woman's mind and actually know if she likes you? How is that possible?

And even if you know that, what are you supposed to do about it?

Some of the answers are in this book. Others will come from talking to women out in the field. This is why I strongly encourage you to do the action steps listed in this book. Get out there and really experience the ideas and techniques I'm talking about. That's when everything comes together. For now, let's talk about some of the biggest signs a woman is attracted to you.

7 HIDDEN BODY LANGUAGE CLUES THAT SHE LIKES YOU

The following clues are based on scientific studies done on the concepts of flirting and on my personal experience. When you start talking to women, you'll notice that these signals come up more often when a woman is interested. The list below is ordered from least to most weighted in terms of interest level. After we go over these clues, I'll show you how to use them.

1. Prolonged Eye Contact

When a woman is looking you in the eyes, that's a good sign she's interested. At the very least, it means she's paying attention to you. Pay attention to this when you're talking to a girl. If she's holding eye contact with you for more than three to five seconds at a time, that means she's engaged in the conversation. The only way you can tell if she's looking you in the eye is if you look in hers. Remember, holding eye contact is part of building tension, so it's a win-win right there.

2. Playing with or Flipping Her Hair

People get fidgety when they're nervous. If a woman is nervous around you, that means she cares about your opinion of her, which means she could be attracted. Since most women have long hair, that's an easy place for them to fidget. A woman will play with her hair by touching it, stroking it, or even twirling it. And since we're on the topic of fidgeting, look out for any other fidgety moves, such as her playing with her necklace or rings.

A woman will also flip her hair behind her head. That's because she wants to expose her neck to you, which is a sign of attraction. Once again, she's showing she cares about the interaction.

3. *Laughing*

Sometimes a woman will laugh when you're funny, and sometimes she'll laugh because she's attracted to you. Women also laugh or giggle out of nervousness. Laughing is a great signal for any of these reasons. Notice when she's laughing. Is she doing it because you're telling a joke, or is it a reflex to your general comments? It's rare that a woman is laughing at you. If she's not interested, she usually puts on a more disgusted face or just leaves the conversation altogether. Watch for laughter or giggling; it's a sign she's enjoying her time with you.

4. *Smiling*

Like laughing, smiling is a sign she likes you and she's enjoying herself. That's what people do when they're having a good time. In fact, smiling is the number one sign a woman is interested in you; however, I'm going to share a few others I believe are more powerful.

5. *Any Physical Contact*

If a woman is purposefully touching you on any part of your body, then pay close attention. Purposeful touching includes reaching out to touch your arm, elbow, hand, or anywhere else that's *not* an accident. I don't want you to think she's interested if she bumps into you or accidentally grazes you when she grabs her drink. We're looking for touch with intention. She's doing this to create a physical connection with you.

6. *Decreased Physical Distance*

Whether you're at a bar or loud club or on the sidewalk, if a woman is getting closer to you during the conversation, that's a great sign. She might be doing it consciously or unconsciously, but this doesn't matter. The mere fact that she doesn't feel threatened or untrusting of you is huge. Look out for her entering your personal space and make sure you don't back off. Stay right where you are and let her get close.

7. Mirroring Your Body Language

In Chapter 2, I mentioned that you want to build tension with a woman by standing face to face as if you're looking into a mirror. If a woman tries to stand face to face with you, take this as a sign. Even more, if she's mirroring your body language, then she's gained rapport with you. That means you've successfully made a connection with her. An example of mirroring might be if you're holding your left hand up and her right hand is doing the same thing, like she's your reflection in a mirror.

Do you need all seven signs to know she's into you? No, you don't. I would look for two or three of these signs to get a good idea if she's interested. For example, maybe she's giving you good eye contact, laughing, and decreasing her physical distance. That combination is a good sign that she likes you.

Wait, but there's more! Body language cues, while powerful, are not the only way to tell if she's interested. There are some verbal clues you should know as well.

VERBAL SIGNS A WOMAN IS INTERESTED IN YOU

She Asks You a Question

Sometimes, talking to a girl is like pulling teeth. She's barely responsive to your questions and she's not chiming in on your statements. This means she's not yet attracted and barely interested. When a girl goes out of her way to ask you a question, that means she has some desire to engage in the conversation with you. It doesn't matter what the question is. As long as she asks you a question, she's interested (except, of course, if she asks, "Can you please go away?").

Compliments

This is a big one. If a woman says anything friendly about you, then she's being nice to you. Don't take this for granted. Women know when and how to show and not show interest. She won't compliment you if she isn't interested in you. In fact, if she compliments you and shows no other verbal or nonverbal sign, this is enough to tell me she's starting to or has already become attracted.

Continuing Conversation

Sometimes, when conversation slows down, the woman you're talking to will chime in to keep it going. Isn't that nice of her? She's doing that because she doesn't want to stop talking to you! Once again, she's not trying to get away from you. Look out for this when you're talking to her. See if she's eager to keep the conversation going and even acting excited about it. This brings me to the next sign.

Her Vocal Tonality

Does she sound excited when she talks to you? Is she talking loudly and with energy? This is a sign of excitement, which could be a sign of interest. On the other hand, she could be very monotone or appear "sleepy" in conversation. That doesn't mean she's *not* interested, but it definitely means she's not very engaged yet. Does her vocal tonality go up at the end of a sentence? That means she's seeking rapport from you and trying to get your attention.

Now, what are you supposed to do with all these signs? They're not there to boost your ego. It means she's interested, so you need to move the interaction forward. Generally speaking, the next move is to see if you can bounce her to a new location (see the section on displaying dominance in Chapter 1). However, let me show you another, very practical way of moving the interaction forward.

GETTING COMPLIANCE AND DISPLAYING DOMINANCE

In Chapter 1, we discussed how dominance is one of the principles of building attraction. Remember, dominance is a masculine trait that turns her on. It's also the driving force that keeps you out of the friend zone. Let's dive deeper into this concept.

From the moment you first talk to her until the moment you enter the bedroom, you want to get *compliance*. This means she's accepting your forward advances as you continue to spend time with her (i.e., she gives you her number, agrees to a date, and so on). I want to give you three key tests that you can use to (a) see if she's interested and (b) move the interaction forward.

The Isolation Test

Whether you meet a woman in a social environment (bar, club) or a casual environment (sidewalk, grocery store), there's always an opportunity to isolate her. The reason for isolating her is to test if she's invested in you. A woman who's invested in you will take the opportunity to be alone with you because she's interested in progressing the interaction. This test will give you an idea of how invested she actually is.

To do this in a social environment, simply let her know you should grab a drink, go to a quieter spot, or get some fresh air. Moving her to a new location is powerful on many levels. First, it gets you compliance, which means she's saying yes to your requests; therefore, it lets you continue moving forward. Second, it builds further investment because she's deciding to spend more time with you and do it in a new location. The best time to do this is after 10-15 minutes of talking to her or after 2-3 signs of interest.

If she's in a casual environment, such as a sidewalk, you can tell her to come with you while you run a quick errand. Or you can ask her on an instant date to a coffee shop nearby. Remember, it's about continuing the interaction and moving it forward one step at a time. The best time to do this is after 10-15 minutes of talking to her or after 2-3 signs of interest.

The Kissing Test

If you're talking to her for a while, you can also test her investment by going in for the kiss. This brings the interaction to a physical level. Ideally, you're going to want to test her willingness to kiss you when you two are isolated. It's not a hard and fast rule to be isolated in order to go for the kiss but 100 percent kiss her if you are. You'll want to close the gap between you two and move closer to her. If she doesn't back away, then that's a sign she'll accept your kissing advance. Create a silence by not saying anything, then lean in for the kiss (more on this in Chapter 7).

The Sex Test

Once she's been isolated and you've kissed, you have a great opportunity to invite her back to your place. A great way to do that is simply letting her know you have some great drinks at your place and you should go back and have one. Another way of getting her back to your place is referencing something that came up in conversation and you have at your place, like an art piece, vinyl records, specific foods, new TV, etc. Having a reason to go back to your place makes it smoother and less awkward as you're moving the interaction forward.

It's important to understand that going back to your place does *not* necessarily mean she wants to have sex. But you've now created the opportunity to do so, which is why you move the interaction to this point. Before you have sex, it's important to get consent (this is described in greater detail in Chapter 7).

What Do You Do If She's Around Friends?

One common issue with being able to isolate the girl your interested in is dealing with her friends. When you're approaching and talking to a specific girl don't completely ignore her friends or your girl might feel uncomfortable leaving them. You don't have to be talking to them for too long to win them over but be nice enough to them so they trust you. If you see that her friends are trying to drag her away or feel completely left out, then get them into conversation for a minute or two. Just remember to go back to talking to your girl so you can continue to build attraction. This balancing act between friends should help when you want to move your girl around the club or bar.

THE IMPORTANCE OF CALIBRATION

At this point, you might be saying to yourself, "Tripp, you make it sound a lot easier than it actually is!" And you're right, because what I'm describing here is a perfect scenario. Of course, things may come up where you won't be able to isolate her, she rejects your kiss, or she won't come back to your place. The entire reason we take small steps forward and get her to comply with your requests is because it takes a woman more time to decide if she wants to sleep with you. You can't go up to a woman on the street and say, "Hey, let's go back to my place and have sex!" She'll say no every single time. But if you slowly move the interaction forward and give her enough time to get to know your personality, then you'll have a much higher chance of success.

With that in mind, you need to calibrate to the situation. Calibration means gauging how she's feeling when she's with you. If she's showing signs she's interested, like I discussed above, then you can get her isolated. If she complies with that, then you have an opportunity to kiss her, and so on. Being able to read how she's feeling (calibration) requires empathy, which is important to this process. Empathy is innate, but you can strengthen it by doing lots of approaches. The more interactions you have, the more in-tune you'll be with her reactions and how she's feeling.

On the other hand, she might not be showing many signs of interest. What are you supposed to do then? Imagine you've been talking to a girl and she's paying attention to you but doesn't seem that interested. She's not looking into your eyes or adding to the conversation. First, good on you for being empathetic and recognizing her disinterest. This was the first step. Now that you've recognized this, calibrate to the situation. Because you know how she's feeling, do something different to build attraction. Perhaps switch topics or face her more in conversation. Try doing something that entertains you so you can get her more engaged. Or try and isolate her to create a new environment for you two.

Calibration also takes place when she's showing lots of interest in you. Because you're aware of her attraction, you'll proceed with moving the interaction forward: isolate to kiss to sex.

If this sounds complicated, then understand that the more you go out and talk to girls, the easier it becomes. The more conversations you have, the more opportunities you have to practice empathy and know when it's okay to move the interaction forward and when not to. When in doubt, try to isolate her and go for the kiss. Getting rejected is the worst thing that can happen. However, with sex, you still always need to get consent. No matter what happens, no means no.

WHAT'S PLAN B?

Let's look at a few different scenarios.

You've been talking to a girl for 10 minutes at a bar. She's laughing at your jokes. She's smiling at you and looking in your eyes. She's very engaged in conversation. You ask her to go to the bar to get a drink (isolation) and she says she has to go back to her friends. What do you do?

Or

You meet a girl at the coffee shop. After talking for 20 minutes, you both head out because you asked her to come run a quick errand with you to get a T-shirt at the mall next door. After you leave the mall, you see if she wants to come to your place to have some dinner. She declines. What do you do?

Or

You approach a woman on the sidewalk and you talk to her for five minutes. She then explains that she has to go. What do you do?

Or

You're at a club and you've been with a woman for an hour. You've been making out and dancing and it's going very well. She's obviously very interested in you. You ask her to come back to your place to have a drink and she declines. What do you do?

There's only one answer to all these situations. **You get her number to set up a date.** Most guys think that's the first goal. It's actually plan B. In the next chapter, I'm going to teach you how to get the number and then how to use it to set up a second meeting.

ACTION STEPS:

• Pick one bar in your city, then start a conversation with a woman. After five or ten minutes, ask her to get a drink with you at the bar, to go outside for fresh air, or to find a spot where it's "not too loud."

• Pick one casual area in your city. Start a conversation with a woman, and after five or ten minutes, ask her if she wants to grab coffee with you or isolate her to run an errand.

• Approach one woman (make these approaches separate from the above two) and try and pick out two or three verbal or nonverbal signs she's interested.

MAGNETIC

CHAPTER 5

HOW TO TEXT A GIRL YOU LIKE (STEAL THESE EXAMPLES!)

If you follow the action steps in this book, you're going to get a lot of numbers. Your phone will be filled with them. That's because it's not always easy to isolate a woman and bounce her to your place. In many instances, you'll end up with her number. What are you supposed to do now?

First, I want you to look at what a number realistically is. A number or even her social media contact is just another way to get in touch with her. It doesn't mean she's necessarily invested or attracted to you. For example, you could be having an amazing night with a woman, spend a whole hour with her, isolate her, make out with her, and try to get her home. She politely declines due to having to be up the next day (poor logistics) and you get her number. You're so excited about this girl! Her lips were amazing when you kissed, you both love the same music, and you're extremely attracted to her. This woman could be your new girlfriend. Wait a minute; she wants to have kids and so do you. She could potentially be your wife. All this excitement only to find out she doesn't answer your text message the next day. Ouch!

This excitement is going to happen multiple times when you get a number, but there's something you need to understand. Women live in the temporary emotions of the moment. When she meets you, at a bar for example, she's caught in a whirlwind of excitement and high energy. The next day, she's a little hungover and lying in bed and thinking about the fact she has work tomorrow. Suddenly, you text her and she's "just not feeling it," so she doesn't text you back. This flakiness happens a lot. The atmosphere in which you first meet her, whether at a bar or grocery store, is much different than when she's home on her couch and just hanging out. She doesn't always think, "I gave him my number so I want to see him again."

> **Instead, she'll see your text message and subconsciously ask herself if she feels invested and interested enough to see you again. This happens while she's in a completely different headspace than when she first met you.**

So if you ever get a woman's number and she doesn't text you back, you can count on a couple things: (a) she gave you a number because she was scared to reject you or (b) you didn't get her invested.

When it comes to A or B, there's nothing you can do but practice abundance mentality (see the next section) and move on. You need to be honest with yourself and learn what you could do better next time. This is called the *growth mindset* because you're focused on doing whatever it takes to get better instead of blaming the woman for rejecting you. For example, maybe you got her number too quickly in the interaction and could have continued talking to her to get more investment. Or maybe you were in a group with her friends and you didn't pay enough attention to her to build attraction. Whatever it is, take an honest look at the conversation and see where you could have done better. This growth mindset will get you more results in the long run.

HOW TO ACHIEVE ABUNDANCE MENTALITY

We briefly covered this in Chapter 1, but I'd like to revisit it because it's one of the main sources of the problems I've seen with my coaching clients over the past 10 years. If you can get this part handled, then you'll have a superpower in your dating and sex life.

Abundance mentality is the mindset and understanding that there are many women available to date, sleep with, and get into relationships with. There are approximately 3.8 billion women in the world. Naturally, not all of those women are available. Some are too young, too old, not single, not in your country, not in your city, or not attractive to you. This lowers the pool a bit. Let's knock that 3.8 billion down to a reasonable number. Let's say, if you never decide to leave your city and only stay in one place forever, you have only 5,000 women available to you. That's 0.00013 percent of the world's female population. To me, that number is on the low end of actual availability but still *extremely* high. Hopefully we can agree on this reasonable number of women available to you.

Imagine if you decided to talk to five women every day. Wow, that's a lot. That adds up to 1,825 women in one year! Realistically, you aren't going to talk to five women every single day for a year.

But if you did, you'd have hit only 37 percent of 5,000, meaning you wouldn't even be able to meet 5,000 in one year. That gives us 3,175 women left for the next year (still assuming you've been talking to five women every single day). Now, let's also assume that more and more people get into relationships every year, so this knocks down the 5,000 women available to you. However, every day a new woman gets *out* of a relationship, so this evens out the score. So by number standards, the number of potentially available single women is very high (and obviously I'm making up numbers here, which only means that the 5,000 number is actually higher).

Now, I get it. Just reading the numbers doesn't necessarily do much justice to one's true abundance mentality. But it's a start. When a man meets a woman he really likes or really connects with, his mind becomes foggy and it's hard for him to imagine liking another woman. His emotions take over and all he can think about is this one special woman he had a connection with. Maybe he got her number at a bar. Maybe he slept with her. Maybe he went on a few dates with her. Maybe she became his girlfriend. Maybe they got married. Maybe they even had kids. It's easy for a man to connect with a woman, fall in love with her, and forget about the possibility of anyone else. On a biological level, this is your brain saying you've found a good partner to mate and raise children with. The primal side of you is craving to stay with this woman. Yet this biological reaction is completely irrational. It doesn't mean there isn't another woman out there for you.

When you become invested in a woman or fall in love with her, remember that your options are *still* available to you. If she doesn't respond to your text, doesn't agree to a third date, breaks your heart after four years of being together, or decides she wants a divorce, that **doesn't mean there's not a woman out there for you.**

I've been in that boat before, so I know what most guys' responses are to that:

"But, Tripp, there's not going to be another one like HER."

And I can't agree more. You're absolutely right. There won't be another woman who looks like her, talks like her, and thinks like her. But you're missing one important aspect: it's not so much what she's like that keeps you attracted.

What keeps you attracted to a woman is the feeling you get when you're with her.

That feeling is in abundance. You can have that feeling again with another woman 100 times over. This is not an opinion; it's a fact. Listen, I consider myself a romantic guy. I appreciate the fact that having this feeling with a woman can be rare. High-quality women who you're attracted to are more common than you think. My clients have proven it time and time again, and I've proven it to myself.

Every time I've been upset, heartbroken, or in the dumps because it didn't work out with a woman, another one came around the corner. And when it didn't work out with her, another one came around the corner. And when it didn't work out with that one, another one came around the corner. I think you get my point.

Most importantly, abundance mentality comes from the fact that you're capable of meeting another woman. Before reading this book, you might have looked at meeting a woman in a more serendipitous way, which means occurring by chance. The good news is, this is no longer your reality. You don't have to wait anymore to meet an amazing woman. You can be proactive and go out right now! Because you now know you can control this area of your life, you understand that if one woman leaves, another one is around the corner.

Now, in order to create true abundance in your life, you need to "do confidence" (revisit "How to Become Instantly Confident" in Chapter 2) by talking to many women and experiencing this for yourself. I can sit here all day with numbers and facts, but going out there and approaching and experiencing women will be the most powerful. So I urge you to do all the action steps in this book to work on this area of your life and meet some of the amazing women this world has to offer.

WHEN AND HOW TO GET HER NUMBER

Let's take a look at an ideal interaction so you can get a sense of how it's all supposed to flow:

Opener (1 min): You approach a woman and get conversation started.

Topic She Loves (2–5 min): You use a topic from chick crack to get conversation going.

Extraction (5–15 min): Here, you're using the extraction method to continue conversation.

Isolation: This is when you bring her to a new location within the venue (i.e., bar) if you're using the social approach or to a different spot in your town (i.e., coffee shop) if you're using the casual approach.

Bounce: This is when you try and bring her to your place or another location after you've spent time with her in isolation.

First Date: This is when you try and see her again if you couldn't bounce her back to your place or another location.

When in the interaction will you get her number? Most guys do it too early, when she's not invested, which ends up in a "flaky number," meaning she won't respond or won't agree to a date. It's better to get it when it's absolutely necessary. Here are the most common situations when you **should** get her number:

1. If you're having a long night out at a bar and meet a woman in the very beginning of the night and don't plan on spending the rest of the night with her because you're just warming up
2. If you're talking to a woman and she has to leave the conversation to meet her friends
3. If you try and bounce her to a different venue/location and she can't come with you

The pattern here is that you want to get her number if she can't continue the interaction from the initial location to the sex location. This is when you grab her number and meet with her another time. Here's my favorite line to ask for her number:

"We should hang out again sometime. Why don't you put your number in my phone."

You can also say:

"You seem cool. I want to see you again some time. Why don't you give me your number and we'll make it happen."

The key is telling, not asking. Telling her and assuming she'd give you her phone number is much more dominant and attractive. The mindset of assuming she'd be interested helps her subconsciously understand that she *is* interested.

After she puts her number in your phone, you can even call her phone to check if she gave you the right number and didn't make a typo. So then you'll say something like this:

"Cool. I'm calling you right now so you have my number. Let me know if you see it coming through."

This is where she'll check her phone to see if it's working and you're calling the right number. If that goes smoothly, you're good to go.

TROUBLESHOOTING GETTING THE NUMBER

The above scenario is an example of the process being frictionless. It's also one in which you know you've probably built enough attraction and investment that she'll want to see you again (of course, you'll only know for sure once you try and text her to meet up).

However, once in a while, you'll have a woman "test" or "tease" you during the process, and it's best to play it off smoothly. She might say to you something like the following:

"How about I get your number instead?"

Translation: You haven't built enough attraction and I'm not that interested.

Never trust a woman when she wants to get your number. In my whole 10 years of meeting women and teaching men, I've never heard of a woman actually calling the guy after meeting him in person. If it happens to you, please email me at tripp@trippadvice.com with legit proof and I'll send you 100 dollars. The point is, this is rare, and I never want you to fall into this trap. If a woman wants to get your number, politely decline because it's pointless. In that situation, I'd say this:

"No, that's okay. I'd rather just call you. But if you don't trust me, then this probably won't work out."

If she changes her mind, great. If not, walk away. This is a great way to get into the abundance mindset because you always want to be in control of the courting process. If she asks for your number, that's equivalent to her rejecting you. And that's okay! Just say goodbye and move on.

A woman might also say something like this:

"Hmm, I'm not sure. I don't even really know you yet."

Translation: She doesn't feel a connection with you due to the lack of attraction.

This is a great response from a woman. She's being upfront and honest about how she feels. It's better than her agreeing to give you her number and then not responding the next day. From here, I'd agree and exaggerate comically:

"You're right. I'm a complete stranger. And you should never give your phone number to strangers! Okay, let's get to know each other. What's your favorite food?"

This is making light of the situation and being playful with her. The point is to not act upset and to continue talking to her for another 10–20 minutes to continue building attraction. If you try again and she still won't give you her number, then count this as a rejection, say nice to meet you, and walk away. Once again, you're practicing abundance mentality. Never try to convince a woman to like you. That's not how attraction works. You attempt to trigger it, and if it doesn't work and there's no connection, just move on! You gave it your best shot.

If she's not interested she may say this:

"Actually, I better not. I just got out of a relationship and…"
"Actually, I better not. I'm not really dating anyone right now…"
"Actually, I better not. I'm just out having fun with my friends tonight…"

Translation: You didn't build enough attraction with me and I'm not interested.

At this point, I'd get into the abundance mindset, say nice to meet you, and move on. And be thankful you didn't get a flaky number.

WHEN TO TEXT A GIRL TO GET HER TO MEET UP

This is one of the oldest questions in dating advice history. When do you ask her out? The answer is very simple: the next day. Why?

Women have a lot of distractions, like social media, work, hobbies, life problems, and other men they're dating. Every day you don't make initial contact she'll slowly lose attraction for you. Remember, attraction happens in person and on a primal, biological level. Distractions and time will slowly make her forget what she felt for you when you first met. That's why you should contact her within 24 hours.

The key is this: if she's attracted and invested in you, she'll be excited to hear from you.

No girl in the history of the world who's been interested in a man has thought, "Ugh, he reached out too soon. Forget this guy!"

Text her the next day and follow the guidelines in the next section.

THE 5 RULES OF TEXTING A WOMAN

Now you have her number. What's the next step? The next step is getting her out on a date. It's not flirting with her or getting to know her over text. You need to ask her out on a date. Let's dive deeper with my most important principles for texting girls.

1. Always be closing: Your first priority should be inviting her on a date. The relationship doesn't begin until you've gone on a date. Chitchatting over text will engage her intellect, but it's not likely to increase her attraction for you. In fact, she's likely to lose interest as you run out of things to text about. Focus on getting her out on the date. Period.

2. Think about things from her viewpoint: Remember, she has other people who are texting her and trying to get her attention, too. Are your texts boring or self-serving? Are they giving her "work" to do? Or are they a welcome distraction? Are you thinking about what would be interesting to her, too?

3. Make her feel something: She makes her decisions based on how she feels in the moment. Does your text make her feel something, or is it just a boring message like "Hey, how's it going?" Give her positive feelings, not just information about you.

4. Metal is easier to bend when it's red hot: When your texts give her a surge of positive emotions, it's much easier to get her to agree to a date. Don't engage her intellect; engage her feelings first. *Then* invite her out on a date.

5. Master the high-status filter: Don't place too much importance on one woman. Act as if you have a dozen other women texting you. This helps reduce needy behavior. Neediness equals women-repellent.

FREE BONUS:
7 DEADLY TEXT MESSAGES SHE CAN'T RESIST!
I have a free gift for you. I've compiled seven of my favorite text messages for every unique situation you'll have with a woman you meet. Whether you're looking for casual sex or a relationship or trying to escape the friend zone or prevent flaking, I'll give you copy/paste texts to send the girl you're texting.

Go to http://www.trippadvice.com/text-girls and get the free video right away. Then continue below to learn more about how to properly text girls to get them to meet up.

THE C.A.R.E. SEQUENCE TO GET HER TO MEET UP

This is your roadmap for knowing exactly what to say at any given point during the "get to know you" process with a girl. This also works well with reviving old numbers that never turned into anything.

The most important thing to remember about the C.A.R.E. sequence is that it *is a sequence* as well as a diagnostic and troubleshooting tool. You've probably never heard of anything like it before, so make sure you take your time and read it twice to absorb this section. It's actually very easy once you understand how it works.

The basic idea is that you always start using step one, which is the "C" phase of the sequence: going for the close. If she agrees to go on a date with you, then you don't need to proceed any further into the sequence at this time. Congratulations, you've succeeded. Let's start by looking more closely at the "C" phase of the sequence.

Phase 1

C = Close (as in "going for the close"): Always start with this. When you get a girl's number, your top priority should be setting up the first date with her. Do *not* try to have a long-winded conversation over text. If you do, you'll find it harder to get her out on a date. Remember, always "invite" her on a date; don't "ask" her on a date. Inviting assumes you have equal status. Asking assumes you have lower status and that you want something from her.

Examples:

I just discovered this new sushi joint downtown. Let's go together sometime this week. You game?

I'm thinking of hitting up the carnival this weekend. Let's go together. I'll win you a prize :p

Hey, do you like dessert? I just discovered this crazy new place. Let's go together this week.

Hey, let's hit up a wine-tasting bar this week. I know a great spot downtown.

The coolest people in town are going to X bar on Saturday. Come with me. Everybody is going to love you.

Hey, Sarah, it's Tripp. Let's continue our chat from last night. How about we grab drinks this week?

Note: You may have noticed that most of these invitations are general, not specific. The reason we start with general invites (like grabbing coffee sometime this week) is because it's easy for her to say yes. Once she says yes to the general idea of going out with you, it's much easier to nail down a day and time that works for both of you. Once she says yes, you can ask her which days she's free this week. Then find a match for free time and propose the specifics of the date.

Warning: Beware of leading with a specific day and time in your initial text, because if she's not free, she has to say no. Too many of those and now you've become the guy she says no to, and it's actually harder for her to say yes psychologically.

Phase 2

If she's not responding to your texts or she's being evasive about nailing down a day and time for the date, shift to the "A" (ask a question). If she responds to "A," work your way *backward* to "C" and go for the close. So the sequence here is "A" and then "C."

A = Asking a question: This is pretty easy. Just ask her a question she can answer without thinking about. If you ask her a thought-provoking question that takes time to answer, she may put it off so she can think about it and then forget to write you back. You want to aim for a fast and easy response.

Here's an example:

You: Hey, weird question. Which is better: dark chocolate or milk chocolate?

Her: Definitely milk chocolate. Why?

You: (This is where you shift back into going for the close) I was thinking of hitting up this gourmet chocolate bar sometime in the next week. Let's go together.

Her: That sounds great actually :)

Here are some more examples:

I just saw two black cats cross my path. Do two bad lucks equal one good luck?

I think I may need to start a new bucket list. What's one of yours?

I'm curious: what's your "go to" video for a laugh?

What weird food combinations do you really enjoy? (Can you tell I'm hungry?)

I need a new app. Which one do you have that I should definitely try?

I'm curious: what are some unusual places you've been to?

Side note: When you say "I'm curious," it softens the question so it doesn't seem like a totally random interview question.

Phase 3

If she's not responsive to the "A," move to the "R," where you remind her of what she saw in you in the first place. Then, once again, work backward through the "A" and then the "C" to get the date. So the sequence here is "R," "A," and then "C."

R = Remind her of what she saw in you in the first place: All you're doing here is getting her to remember why she liked you and wanted to stay connected with you. If you initially connected while flirting and bantering, then you can send her a flirty text or a funny GIF or meme. If you both love ethnic food, tell her something awesome you're eating.

Example:

You: Hey, I'm cooking some Indian food tonight. Do you like to cook?

Her: I love Indian food! I can't cook it, but I can eat it… lol.

You: I actually know an amazing place to get Indian street food. How about we go together sometime this week?

Her: Really? I'd love to!

More examples:

I'm making my grandmother's fettuccine recipe and it smells amazing, but I need your help. Red or white wine?

So I'm curious: what's your favorite thing about growing up in [insert place]?

Hey, I'm curious: what's the best trip you've been on? I'm heading to Ireland next week (first time).

I'm learning to play guitar from a video game (I'm gonna be famous!). Play any instruments?

Everybody on Earth has a secret nerdy hobby. I love to read trashy science fiction. What's yours?

Let's play a game :) - What's a secret you normally wait to tell until the third date but wish you could say on the first?

Phase 4 (Final Phase)

And finally, if none of the first three steps work to get her on a date, deploy the final phase of the sequence, which is the "E," where you eliminate possible excuses and get her on the phone. So the sequence here is "E," "R," "A," and then "C" (which is C.A.R.E. spelled backward).

E = Eliminate excuses: Use this only when there's been a lot of difficulty in getting her to schedule a date. Simply use one of the texts from Phase 2 or 3 (the "A" and the "R" stage of the C.A.R.E. sequence, respectively). When she responds, call her right away because she already has her phone in hand and she's more likely to pick up. Then you can schedule the date.

Examples: (These texts force a reply. When she replies, call her right away.)

I just saw the weirdest thing.

Do you have a twin sister?

I can't believe what just happened.

Do you have emergency training?

Were you just at the [insert place here]?

I just met a girl who looks exactly like you downtown!

Do you have a younger sister working at the movie theater in the west end?

Warning: You can only do this once or twice. A tactic known is a tactic blown. Eventually she'll see that you're trying to force a response so you can call her, and she'll resent you for it. Only use this tactic when nothing else has worked. Think of it as a last-ditch effort before you forget about her and move on.

How to Use the C.A.R.E. Sequence

The main thing to remember is that you only need to move to the next step in the sequence if the step you're using right now isn't getting the response you want. Then, once you *do* get the response to whatever phase of the sequence you're in, you work your way *backward* to the "C."

I know this is a lot to take in at first, but I promise this is very easy. It's like learning to drive. At first, it's confusing to deal with the steering wheel, gas, brake, signals, other cars, etc., but eventually it becomes second nature. The C.A.R.E. sequence is insanely easy to understand once it clicks in your mind. Just stick with it and you'll wonder how you ever texted girls without knowing this.

To make things easier, use this flowchart for reference.

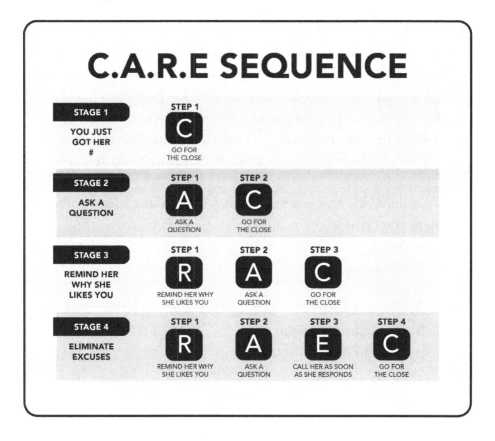

THE BEST FIRST DATE IDEAS

Let's make this very simple. The best first date is you and her going to a bar and getting a couple drinks. It's simple, easy, and affordable, and it gives you the best chance to continue building attraction. Pick a spot close to your place or hers so it gives you a chance to continue the date. Personally, I like to pick a wine bar that's dim lit and has a chic vibe to it. Lounges are a great place to do this.

If you don't drink or you're underage, here's a quick list of other things you can do:
- tea/coffee
- bowling/mini-golf
- museum
- amusement park
- frozen yogurt/ice cream
- trivia night (minus the drinks)

Don't overthink it. Just find something that lets you talk and be physically close with one another. I would stay away from anything that prevents talking, like movies, concerts, or seminars. Those don't allow you to connect.

In the next chapter, I want to go over how to plan a date with a woman and get physical with a woman to the point of sex. When you know these techniques, it'll be easy to transition to sex. For now, here are the action steps to continue your approaching.

ACTION STEPS:

Go to http://www.trippadvice.com/text-girls and download a free video that talks about the seven deadly text messages she can't resist.

If you're texting with any woman right now, immediately follow the C.A.R.E sequence and try to get her on a date.

Pick one bar in your city, start a conversation with one girl, and after five or ten minutes, use the closing line to get her number: *"Let's hang out again sometime. Put your number in my phone."*

Note: you can still move forward with isolation and bounce, but I want you to practice the motions of getting her number. Also, don't worry if you don't get the number. The point is to practice.

Pick one casual area in your city, start a conversation with one girl, and after five or ten minutes, use the closing line to attempt getting her number.

Note: you can still move forward with isolation and bounce, but I want you to practice the motions of getting her number. Also, don't worry if you don't get the number. The point is to practice.

If you're successful with any numbers, use the C.A.R.E. sequence and ask her on a date.

— ∽ —

CHAPTER 6

FIRST DATES THAT LEAD TO SEX

I'm going to let you in on a little secret. You ready? Women like sex.

In fact, they *love* sex.

That entire concept will change the way you view meeting and seducing women. When you understand that women want to have sex with you, then you'll be making different types of decisions, because I guarantee you're not operating under that paradigm right now.

First, how do I know that women like sex? Look at any modern magazine like *Cosmopolitan.* Half of the headlines are about how to have better sex or how to give him the best sex of his life. Also, women tell me they like sex. Make any girl a friend and have an open and candid conversation on the topic. They'll let you in and tell you how much they enjoy having sex. If you've ever had a girlfriend, maybe you know that truth as well. You were probably having sex as much as you wanted. They're horny, just like you, dude.

Then why don't women jump into bed with every man they meet? And how come they won't have sex as quickly a man will? That's because of something called "slut shaming." And it really is a damn shame. Society has a double-standard that says it's cool for guys to have lots of sex but it's not cool when women have lots of sex. Men are called "players" when they sleep with a lot of women, and women are called "sluts." I wish I could change that double-standard and give all women permission to do what they want with their bodies without the fear of guilt, shame, or judgment, but that's just not the world we live in (at least in America).

Also, having sex is much more risky for women than it is for men. They can get pregnant! So as much as they want to have sex, they're biologically wired to mate with the man who knows how to pull her attraction triggers (which you've been learning how to do). She's waiting for the man to display his masculine personality traits that tell her he's someone she should sleep with. Moreover, she's looking for the man that makes her feel emotionally safe and not judged. The minute she feels judged or shamed for her sexual desires, she gets turned off. Society has a great hold on women's promiscuity, so it's your job to lead her to the bedroom safely and seductively.

3 HACKS TO HAVE AN AMAZING FIRST DATE

If you followed the C.A.R.E. sequence outlined in the previous chapter, you should be able to set up the first date. You either picked an activity or a nice chic lounge to have a drink. Here's a few tips to optimize the date for success:

Show Up Five Minutes Early

It looks good if you're on time, and I'm sure you expect the same out of your date, too. Nobody likes having their time wasted. Also, if you're early and grabbing a drink, you can pick the best spot in the place. The best spot to pick is at the bar. It allows you two to be close to each other. The next best spot is at a small table or booth.

Pay for the First Date

One of the most debated topics in dating advice literature is who should pay on the first date. I'm going to make this easy for you: you do it. You're the one who asked her out. Paying and taking control of the bill displays a masculine quality, and she'll appreciate it. If she reaches for the bill, that's a good sign you have a good woman on your hands. Politely tell her you'll get this one and she can get the next. Don't be cheap and just take care of it, because you'll score bonus points.

Hug Her for the Greeting

You want the date to start off on a physical note and to let her know this isn't a business meeting. So don't shake her hand. And no high-fives. You want to set the tone that you're a guy who's comfortable with touching. Break the touch barrier right away and give her a hug. No exceptions.

WHAT ARE YOU SUPPOSED TO TALK ABOUT ON A FIRST DATE?

There's not much of a difference between the first interaction and the first date. Your job on the first date is twofold: qualify her for relationship material if you're looking for a girlfriend and build attraction. That's it. I'll teach you in Chapter 8 how to qualify her for relationship material, but let's recap how to build attraction.

Building Sexual Tension

Hold consistent eye contact with her and don't slouch. Make sure you're speaking in downward tonality as to have a more masculine and commanding tone. If you're sitting at the bar, try and face her at a 45-degree angle so you're almost completely facing her. Tip: from time to time, continue breaking the touch barrier by lightly touching her knee or arm when you're making a point in conversation.

Providing Entertainment

Remember, you're supposed to provide entertainment for yourself. What do *you* want to talk about? What's interesting to *you*? At the end of the day, this is the time to just relax and have an enjoyable evening with a stranger. Don't feel you have to do something that's interesting for her. What's interesting to you?! That's what the conversation should be like. Tell her what you're up to in life. Tell her what's on your mind. Ask her questions you're interested in knowing the answer to, or reference Chapter 3 to find the questions that make a woman feel deeply connected to you.

Displaying Dominance

Lead the conversation. If things get silent for too long, come up with something to say. This shouldn't be a problem, because you learned the extraction method in Chapter 3, which helps keep the conversation going. Take control and order the drinks when she tells you what she wants. If you're not at a bar and doing an activity instead, find the opportunity to take the lead. Using the other date ideas from the previous chapter, here's what leading looks like:

Date: Ice cream/frozen yogurt
Leading: After you order, pick the seat you're going to sit at.

Date: Amusement park
Leading: Tell her which rides you want to go on and go do them.

Date: Bowling
Leading: Help her pick a bowling ball.

Be decisive. Decisiveness is an attractive masculine trait, so take advantage of it wherever possible.

Also, dominance means leading the interaction to the bedroom and beyond. Next, let's talk about how to lead her there from a first date.

LEADING HER TO THE BEDROOM

Remember, women want to have sex (studies even shown they get more pleasure out of it than you, due to the number of nerve endings in the clitoris). She just needs you to safely lead her to that point. It'll take baby steps to get her to the point where she feels comfortable and attracted enough to go through with it. Remember, it's not that she doesn't want to have sex; she just doesn't want to feel like a slut for doing it. It's more comfortable for her to feel like "it just happened."

Assuming everything went well on your date and you used the principles of attraction, then you have a higher chance of bringing her home that night. Your best bet is to find a bar or activity that's close to your apartment or home. If you want to bring her back there after a date, just mention something to do back at your place and escalate from there. Here are some examples:

- See if she wants to have another glass of wine from a special bottle you have.
- Tell her to come watch the funny Netflix stand-up comedy special you mentioned earlier.
- Say you're hungry and make a delicious gourmet macaroni and cheese.

Mixing and matching anything in that vein should work just fine if you properly built attraction.

Remember, many women are interested in having sex, but you won't know that if you don't try, because women are counting on you to make the first move. However, she may not be interested in having sex with you so quickly. Sometimes, you can do all the right steps and she's just not ready yet. That's okay. Don't push it. If she says no, then no means no.

3 IMPORTANT THINGS TO KNOW BEFORE YOU HAVE SEX

1. Will she become more invested in you after sex?

Yes, 100 percent. Once she's having sex with you, she's more invested, which means it's easier to bring it to relationship status or just a consistent casual hook-up. Understand that it's in a woman's biology to become more attached to a man after she has sex. After sex, there's a chemical released called oxytocin, which helps to bond two people together. She'll get attached to you after sex, especially if it's good sex (more on that in Chapter 7). While getting her invested is great, it can also be difficult for some men to deal with. Be warned that she'll be calling you, texting you, and reaching out more often. Don't sleep with a woman if you're not interested in that happening.

2. Should you wear a condom?

Yes. Don't be stupid. Two of the worst things have the possibility of happening if you don't use a condom. You either get a woman pregnant or you get an STI (sexually transmitted infection)—or both. These have the potential to permanently affect your life. I understand that, in the moment, condoms suck and it feels better to do it without one, but you won't ever regret using a condom once the deed is finished. It's only your reptilian, irrational brain that convinces you not to use one in the heat of the moment. So unless she's 100 percent taking birth control and has shown you proof of her STI panel, then use a condom. Even then, please proceed with caution, because no prevention is 100 percent effective.

To find out if she has any STI's simply say to her, "Hey, before we go any further we should talk about our history. Do you have any STI's?" It seems direct but it's better to not beat around the bush and get to the point. And if you have one then you should answer the question after she does and be upfront with her about what you have. If you do have an STI than my advice is to be prepared to answer any questions she may have to make her feel comfortable. And don't be ashamed of it either. The more cool you are with it the higher chances of her being cool with it.

3. How do you get consent?

Consent is very important in the sexual courting process. Why should you do it? First, it's the right thing to do. You don't want to have sex with anyone who isn't completely interested and willing. It's just plain wrong. Second, you could potentially get in a lot of trouble if you don't get a "sober, enthusiastic yes." Anything other than that is grounds for getting into trouble with the law. She must not be intoxicated by drugs or alcohol and must be very interested in having sex by giving you verbal consent. Here's two great ways to ask for consent:

"Hey, I want to make sure we're on the same page here. Do you want to have sex?"

"Should I get a condom?"

Both work well and get the job done. The best time to say one of these two lines is at the point when you're very close to having sex. That means you've been making out for a while, your clothes are potentially off already, or she's been dry humping you. It's better to ask for consent when she's already turned on; otherwise, you risk making it awkward or uncomfortable. It's best to ask when you're already hot and heavy.

In the next chapter, I'll teach you how to blow her mind in the bedroom. First, I'll teach you how to sexually escalate with her and then do the number one move that makes her want to come back for more.

ACTION STEPS:

• Pick one dim-lit or chic bar you could get a drink at with your future date (if not applicable, find the closest place to it).

• Pick one activity to do for a date that's closest to your place.

• Find something interesting in your apartment that you can use to invite a woman over to your place, such as a Netflix special, a nice bottle of wine, a gourmet food recipe, wall art, a new television or tech gadget, or a unique item.

CHAPTER 7:

HOW TO MAKE A GIRL SQUIRT IN UNDER 3 MINUTES!

There's a very fine line between what makes a good or bad sexual experience. In this chapter, I'll teach you how to physically escalate to the bedroom and share a technique that women really enjoy. Many men fail in the department of sex, so it's very easy to stand out and give her and yourself a very pleasurable experience. And if you do this correctly she'll want to come back for more.

HOW TO KISS A GIRL AND MAKE HER WANT MORE

Once you have a girl isolated or she's back at your apartment, you're going to be the one who goes for the kiss. It's very rare that a woman will initiate because she's waiting for you to lead. Remember, she wants a man who's in control and dominant. The best way to initiate a kiss is to be physically close to her and then create a silence. Guys get very nervous due to the fear of rejection. Just remember that it's not going to happen if you don't try.

First, make sure you're close to her in conversation—at the most one foot away. This makes it easy to go for the kiss since your face is close to hers. Second, in order to create a silence, you just have to stop talking. Eventually, the woman you're with will do the same. And after two or three seconds (at the most), you lean in and kiss her. If she doesn't stop talking, you can say this:

"Hold on one second..."

She'll then stop talking and you can lean in for the kiss. Now you have no excuses and you just go for it. If she rejects you, that just means you haven't built enough attraction. Don't fret! Just look her confidently in the eyes and say, "That's okay, you're not ready yet." This says to her exactly what she's thinking but also leaves it on the table to try again in the future. I recommend you try kissing her again in another 20 minutes, after you've continued talking. Sometimes she needs to feel more comfortable. If you get rejected again, just try another time when you see her next.

The big rule to kissing is soft and slow. You only go fast when you've been going at it for a while or already having sex. She'll get more turned on when you aren't so overeager. Use minimal to no tongue and caress her lips with yours. No woman has ever complained when a man kisses slow—only when he goes too fast and shoves his tongue down her throat. This slow speed is going to feel very sensual and keep her wanting to kiss you. You can also kiss for 30 seconds, stop to talk to her again, kiss for another 30 seconds, stop and talk to her again, and then kiss for another one or two minutes. The stopping and starting is a great way to build up the sexual tension and make you come off as non-needy.

I invite you to check out "Tripp's Tension Technique," where you'll see a live video demonstration of me building tension with a beautiful woman. Check it out here: http://www.trippadvice.com/tension-technique. I go through, step by step, the technique of building sexual tension, which turns her on and gets her wanting to kiss you.

HOW TO GO FROM KISS TO SEX

Once you're at your apartment or hers and you've broken the kissing seal, the next steps are just moving forward and going slow. The slower you go, the more you'll turn her on, which in turn makes her want you more. Rushing to have sex is a bad idea because women need time to warm up, just like they need time to feel attracted to you. The faster you go, the more likely she isn't ready and the greater the chance of rejection. Women get turned on by tension more than anything else. It's your job to build that tension, which means going slow.

Here's an easy guideline to create maximum tension when you're with a woman. This will help give you some structure once you've started kissing.

WARNING: If at any moment she seems uncomfortable or says she's uncomfortable or says anything related to no, such as "stop" or "don't," then stop immediately. This is her conveying she's not interested in pushing further. The next move is for you to stop all actions and say, "I only want to do what's comfortable for you. What is comfortable for you right now?" At that point, let her speak and go from there. You shouldn't do anything to make a woman feel uncomfortable, and it's best for your safety to only go further with what you *both* agree upon.

Kissing: Kiss her slowly for at least five to ten minutes. Build the kissing up to the point where she's really enjoying it. You'll know she's enjoying it: if you pull back, she'll come forward to continue kissing you. Hold her tightly, and once in a while, take your hand and put it on her cheek as you're kissing her. This creates a much more sensual vibe.

Moving Her on Top of You: Assuming you're are on a couch, this is a good time to move her on top of you. Ideally, she's straddling you. You'll want to be in this position for another five to seven minutes, kissing and grinding. This will turn you both on, especially her, since you two are simulating sex.

Fondling: Next, you want to start touching her in the more sensual, sensitive spots, such as her breasts and then down near her vagina. Remember, your clothes are still on, but she can still feel these sensations through them. Rub and caress very gently because it's more sensitive than if you're doing it too fast. Too much friction in those spots in the very beginning doesn't help build the tension you're trying to create.

Clothes: After about 10 minutes or so of grinding while she's on top of you, you can start to take off her clothes. I would start with her shirt and then her bra. Continue making out with her, slowly moving down to her neck and then kissing her breasts. This is a super sensitive spot for a woman, so you're continuing to build more sexual tension.

Move to the Bedroom: It's most comfortable to have sex in a bed, so after about five to ten minutes of making out and fondling on the couch, stand up. She'll stand up with you. While standing up, continue making out for a minute, then either pick her up or grab her and go into the bedroom. Put her on the bed and get on top of her. Continue to kiss her and start to take off your clothes, starting with the shirt. After you're kissing for another few minutes, take off her pants and then yours. At this point you should both be just in your underwear, you on top of her and grinding as if you're having sex. This further builds tension before you're actually having sex.

Now, you have a few options at this point. You can either take off her underwear and put your fingers inside of her or you can go down on her. This will turn her on even more. At this point, you can ask for consent to have sex. Or you can skip all that and go right to consent.

Consent: Read "How Do You Get Consent?" in Chapter 6. Here's a quick recap of what you can say:

"Hey, I want to make sure we're on the same page here. Do you want to have sex?"

Or

"Should I get a condom?"

From here, see how she responds, and please respect what she's comfortable doing from here.

HOW TO MAKE A GIRL SQUIRT IN 3 MINUTES!

There's one bedroom move that tops them all: the ability to make a woman squirt (aka female ejaculation). This is a very special move because it's one of the ultimate orgasms for women. When you can successfully perform this technique, it opens up her entire world of sexual possibilities because it's a very unique sensation (and a great one at that).

The reality is, not every woman is going to be able to squirt. Every woman has the *ability*, but sometimes it takes many, many tries to get it right. The good news is, the technique feels very good for a woman whether she can ejaculate or not. Once a woman has had this orgasm once, you can get her to ejaculate within three to five minutes on subsequent tries. It's not a difficult technique to perform; it just takes practice, patience, and trust.

First, let's focus on the technique. Then I'll help you set up the context in which it occurs. Both are equally important in this process.

To perform this technique correctly, get her lying on a bed, preferably far to one side. If you're a righty and use your right hand for most activities, you'll want to have her on the left side of the bed and vice versa for a lefty. Give yourself enough room to sit down on the bed beside her. Take your two middle fingers and put them in her vagina. Your pinky and pointer finger will be pointed downward and grasping onto her butt cheeks for support. (figure 1)

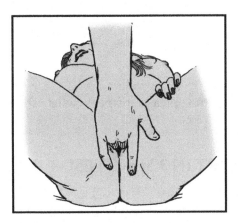

Figure 1

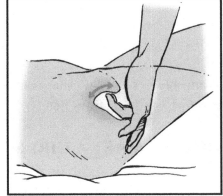

Figure 2

When your fingers are inside her, make a "come hither" motion as if you were signaling someone to come near you. (figure 2) The spot is about two or three inches in. As you curl your fingers in the "come hither" motion, you should feel the G-spot. It's on the upper wall of her vagina, and you're going to feel a soft spot that, when aroused, will have a sponge-like texture. When the G-spot has frequent stimulation, it causes her to have a G-spot orgasm, which is then responsible for her ejaculation. Now, let's go through the technique step by step.

First, you want to make a slow "come hither" motion to lightly arouse the G-spot. After doing this for about a minute, speed up the pace. After another minute, tense up all the muscles in your arm and use your entire arm as a lever to vigorously shake and pump the G-spot. You'll find that this technique makes your arm quite tired, especially if this is her first time, which can potentially take a while. The soreness and built-up lactic acid in your arm from shaking and pumping is normal. In fact, if that's not happening, you might not be doing it hard enough. The vagina is a very strong muscle, so don't be afraid to do this, because she can absolutely handle it. Of course, be aware of her reactions. Ask from time to time how it's feeling. Depending on her verbal communication or her body language, you'll get a feel of whether to slow down or speed up. As always, if she wants you to stop, then you stop. If you're doing it right, she won't want you to stop.

At this point, she may be shaking, moaning, and going wild. Whatever you do, don't stop. Finally, she'll end up ejaculating, which will look like a clear, thin liquid that expels from her urethra. According to studies, the liquid that comes out is very diluted urine. Don't be grossed-out. Most of the liquid is in fact prostatic secretions, which fill up when a woman is aroused. When she's able to release this fluid, it sparks the biggest orgasm a woman can have. As she's releasing the fluid, don't stop until it ends, so she can finish. Don't be surprised if the woman starts laughing maniacally. The produced feeling can be very emotional for women because it opens them up physically and sensually.

Before you use the technique, you need to set up the context for performing this move. It's not as simple as putting her on the bed and going at it. Because of the intensity of the move, you need to let her know what's going on. Women are very self-conscious about their bodies, and in order for them to want to squirt liquid out of their vaginas in front of a man, she has to know she won't be judged for it. The second she tenses up and feels shame, then the technique doesn't have a chance at working. Here's a formula to follow to set the context and make her feel comfortable.

Communication: Tell her you know a move in the bedroom that's supposed to be very pleasurable. When she asks what it is, tell her it's a way to make her ejaculate. If she doesn't believe it's true, then let her know it's a very real thing. If she claims it's just women peeing, then let her know about a study that showed it's mostly liquid from the prostate and only a negligible amount of urine. You don't need to convince her, but she must be somewhat interested in this process before it happens, because you both have roles in the technique. It's very difficult to "accidentally" make a woman squirt. She has to be in on it and consent to the whole process.

Trust factor: After she shows interest, communicate to her that you're very interested in performing it for her and that you won't be grossed out or think it's weird when she ejaculates. You can even mention that it's a beautiful thing. Also let her know you'll stop if she ever gets uncomfortable during the process. However, confirm with her a few times that you won't judge her for anything that happens and you'll respect any outcome, whether she ejaculates or not. Both of you shouldn't look at it like a "goal" to squirt because you don't want to end up disappointed. Look at it more as a fun sexual experiment.

Setup: In order to do this properly, she has to be very aroused and comfortable with what's about to happen. Before you perform this technique, I highly recommend you give her one or two orgasms with cunnilingus, sex, or both. It's better if she's already opened up and turned on. I recommend being intimate with her for at least 30 minutes prior to the move. Have a towel nearby you can put under her butt and vagina for easy clean-up once she ejaculates.

Direction: This next step is important because it's where you really take the lead. Tell her to move to one edge of the bed. Make sure she's completely naked, which she should be if you've been intimate with her. Give yourself enough space next to her so you're able to firmly stimulate her G-spot. Ask her if the temperature is okay and if she's comfortable. We need her very relaxed for this to work, because a woman's anxious thoughts can sabotage this move. It won't work if she's overthinking it. After she's comfortable, reassure her that you're just having fun, whether this works or not. Tell her not to focus on the outcome and to instead focus on the pleasure of your hand and the feeling in her body.

When she's at ease, kiss her and start rubbing your hands on her clitoris. She should already be wet from her previous aroused state. Note: she must be lubed up, so do not perform this if she isn't naturally wet or if there isn't lubrication around. A water-based lubricant or coconut oil works great. Let her know that the sensation of having to pee is 100 percent normal and means it's working. Her bladder is supposed to fill up with liquid during this process. When she feels the urge to pee, tell her to just let it go. Reassure her as many times as you can that this is not urine and is female ejaculate, which will feel amazing once released. This part of the process is extremely important because a woman's self-consciousness of releasing liquid from her urethra will prevent her from having the orgasm.

Once you're inside of her with your fingers and start to perform the technique, don't be afraid to ask her a few times how it feels. Let her know from time to time how beautiful she is and how amazing she smells and how amazing her pussy feels. These compliments will help her feel relaxed, which is key. As soon as you go faster and she's enjoying it, she's going to tell you that she feels it coming. This is when you direct her to ejaculate by saying this:

"Good girl. Go ahead and come. Come for me."

"Push it, baby. Push it out and let it happen."

"Keep going. You're doing great, baby."

Use those lines or improvise, but it's important to verbally guide her through the process so she successfully ejaculates and feels comfortable doing so.

This could take anywhere from three to thirty minutes. It might not happen at all. That's okay! Every woman is different. Remember, she has the ability to do it, but some women need to be more comfortable and have more time to understand her body's reaction to this technique. As long as you're patient and attentive, it should work. And if it does, don't be surprised if she begs you to do it again. This technique has been known to save relationships because it connects two people on a whole new level due to the intimacy of the shared experience.

HOW TO LEARN SEX FROM PORN

Porn.

You probably watch it, and there's a good chance you already watched it today. Don't worry; it's normal. So since you're already watching it, we might as well kill two birds with one stone and learn a few things. I don't believe that watching porn more than a few times per week is healthy because it can desensitize you during sex. However, there are some things you can take away from porn that help you with your sex life. Just remember, watching porn every day can have an addictive effect on our brain that makes it difficult to enjoy sex and even causes erectile dysfunction. So please watch in moderation. But while you're watching, let's see what else can we take away from it besides an orgasm.

Find Out What's Possible

While porn is geared toward achieving the highest form of fantasy for the viewer, there are still positions and moves that women enjoy. When you're watching, take note of what's happening in the scene. How's he holding her? What's he doing? What moves is she doing? These ideas can lead you to discover something you enjoy and never thought of before. One good thing about porn is that it can open up your sexual appetite to something you've never seen, heard of, or experienced before.

Porn also helps you understand that women like to be kinky! You'll see certain sex positions, toys, gadgets, and roleplay that women enjoy doing in real life. Of course, every woman is different, but understand that each woman has a specific sexual appetite. Many women are open to exploring their sexual worlds with men who introduce them to these new things. As long as they feel safe and not judged, then it's a major turn-on for women. Just remember that porn is best used to learn the kinkier stuff, not the actual act of sex in general. The act of sex on camera is a bit more fabricated so it can be caught perfectly on screen.

Also, use porn to connect to the idea of being uninhibited. Let yourself be open to new things and to trying new things in the bedroom. Don't be ashamed of your sexuality and the possibilities of expanded sexual horizons. It may open a new world for you and and help you understand yourself on a deeper level.

Just remember, anything new you want to try with a woman in

the bedroom should be communicated first. Don't ever assume a woman likes something kinky. First, openly talk to her about it and tell her you're interested. The more comfortable you feel with it, the more she will, too. Give her a safe space to tell you if she's interested in exploring this with you. The best way to do this is to bring up what you like in the bedroom in a confident way. And let her know that she can feel comfortable telling you what she likes too.

A note on big penises in porn. First, the camera makes everything look bigger. Also, these are hired actors who are well endowed and highly above average. Don't feel intimidated or insecure if you don't have a penis as big as the ones you see on screen. Most women are fine with a small average size penis and focus a lot on the connection between her and the person she's having sex with. This is what brings her the most pleasure.

ACTION STEPS:

Get my famous "Tripp's Tension Technique" to see a live demonstration of building sexual tension: http://www.trippadvice.com/tension-technique.

Reread the escalation sequence and go through the steps in your head so you remember what to do once you have a woman over at your place.

Reread the squirting sequence and go through the steps in your head so you remember what to do when you have a woman in your bed.

CHAPTER 8:

HOW TO ASK A GIRL TO BE YOUR GIRLFRIEND (AND GET A YES!)

It's rare for a woman to meet a Magnetic Man or a man who understands a woman and how she's thinking and feeling. It's rare for a woman to have an interesting conversation with a confident man who knows how to please her in the bedroom. Most men don't learn how to become a better version of themselves. But you, my friend, are doing that by reading this book and applying the exercises. And when a woman gets the chance to meet a man like you, getting her to be your girlfriend is easy. That's because she'll want to spend a lot of time with that kind of man. You are a man of value.

CREATING THE RELATIONSHIP YOU SEEK

Most men think relationships are one way: monogamous. It's you and a woman and you two are together and that's how it goes. These days it doesn't have to be that way if you don't want it to be. You can create any kind of relationship you desire. There's just two rules to making that happen. First, you have to know the kind of relationship you're looking for, and second, you must communicate this to the woman very early on. Let's go over these rules and how to successfully work through them.

Knowing What Type of Relationship You Want

The opportunities are endless in terms of finding the relationship you want. In fact, I'll make a quick list of the most popular right here:

Monogamous Relationship: You and one woman are committed to one another.

Open Relationship: You and the woman are committed; however, you're each allowed to be sexual with other people.

Threesomes: You and a woman are looking for a third woman for a sexual experience.

Polyamorous Relationship: You and the woman are together but you're allowed to have sexual and emotional connections with other people (i.e., have other boyfriends or girlfriends).

Triad Relationship: You're in a committed relationship with two other women.

Non-Relationship: You're not open to committing to any one partner and are free to have multiple sexual partners.

Understand that this is not a complete list and I have in fact generalized the options just to give you a brief overview. There are even more ways to have a relationship, and I leave that completely to you. You can create whatever you want. Most men are black and white: looking for a monogamous relationship or are sleeping around and in a non-relationship. That's perfectly fine, too. Maybe you're not labeling yourself as anything because you're in discovery mode and finding out what's most suitable for you.

What's most important is that you start with the end in mind. I'd figure out what you're looking for so you can achieve it. For example, if you're looking for a monogamous relationship, search for a partner who's a good fit (more on that in just a bit). If you're looking for an open relationship, you need to communicate that to the woman you started dating so she understands the expectations.

What doesn't work is dating a woman for a while, then, somewhere down the road, saying you want to be in a polyamorous or open relationship. Most likely, she won't be interested and she'll walk out the door—not because there's anything inherently wrong with polyamory, but because that's not what she signed up for. If she knew earlier, she would have let you know she's not interested in that, and you would have parted ways.

My advice is to figure out what you're looking for and start with the end in mind. When you know what type of relationship you want, whether it's monogamy, poly, or nothing, you can act accordingly. The good news is that the formula for attraction doesn't change based on the relationship you want. You still follow the steps outlined in the previous chapters to build attraction, get them invested, build a connection, and have an amazing sexual experience. From there, you'll want to communicate to them what you're looking for in a relationship. That way, you waste no time and stick with your goal.

THE 3 NON-NEGOTIABLES

I'd imagine most men reading this are eventually looking for a monogamous relationship in which you and the woman are committed to each other. This usually comes after a man has experienced sleeping with multiple women and wants to settle down or even have a family. This can also occur after a man dabbles in open or polyamorous relationships. Either way, since most men want a loyal, loving girlfriend, I want to teach you how to choose your three non-negotiables.

These three non-negotiables, aka "deal breakers," are what you need to figure out *before* you end up dating a lot of women. These are the three things you're looking for that qualify a woman to spend time with you. It's your job to find out if she possesses them. The reason you want to have three non-negotiables is to save time. Just dating a woman solely based on looks and sexual chemistry (which many men do) is a recipe for disaster. If you find out she's not the type of woman you really respect or get along with, you may stay in the relationship because you're physically attracted to her. This will be a terrible relationship.

On the other hand, it's also trouble if you're dating a woman who has a great personality match for you (laugh together, interested in the same things, etc.) but you're not very physically attracted to her or you have poor sexual chemistry together. Eventually, your sex life may die and you'll be interested in other women. Understandably, in any long-term relationship, looks fade as we age, but by that point you've grown such a strong bond together that your sex life has the ability to evolve with it. So with that, a long relationship is still possible.

Now, let's talk about how to figure out your non-negotiables.

What's important to you? What would you like in a woman? I want you to think long and hard about what you'd want your partner to be like. Here are some questions you can ask yourself:

Does she have your same sense of humor?
Is she good with children?
Is she financially responsible?
Does she believe in the same god as you?
Is she physically fit?
Does she want children?
Is she over or under a certain age?
Is she open to threesomes?
Is she passionate about her work?
Does she have a lot of friends?
Does she like to be adventurous?
Is she a bookworm?

Now, I bet someone will read these questions and say they want all of those things! However, if you have a list of 20 non-negotiables, you're not realistically going to find this woman because the odds are quite small she exists. This process is most helpful to you if you're realistic and find three non-negotiables. It'll still be difficult to find a woman who has three, so imagine having 20!

Now, it's important to understand that a woman doesn't have to be your girlfriend just because she has these three qualities. It just means she qualifies to continue dating you. She passes your test. Of course, you need to see if you have a sexual connection, you get along, and if you genuinely respect her. If the sex is bad, you don't enjoy your time with her, and she doesn't seem like a woman who has her life together, it's probably not going to last long. More importantly, it definitely won't last long if she doesn't have your three non-negotiables.

HOW DO YOU KNOW WHAT YOUR 3 NON-NEGOTIABLES ARE?

What's important to you? These three non-negotiables might change over time. Someday you might find that one of them isn't important anymore. No problem! Find something else to replace it. As long as you continue always having three set in stone, you'll be practicing mindful dating, meaning you'll always be trying to match with the right person. Personally, it took me a few relationships to figure out what my non-negotiables were, but if I thought about this process way before my previous relationships, I might have not wasted so much time.

My advice is to list out 20 different qualities that are important for you in a relationship. Maybe you know these from past relationships, or maybe you know what you're attracted to in a woman. My advice is, if you want children, then one of them has to be "enthusiastically wants to have children." You don't want to start getting serious with a woman only to find out she "sorta wants to be a mom." That's something you both need to be on the same page about because it will clearly define your future. Here are some other examples:

- physically fit
- responsible with finances
- enjoys traveling
- her own business
- passionate about something
- laughs at similar jokes as you
- reads the same books as you
- has the same religion
- has the same political beliefs

Now, this is just a short list, and it's only meant to give you examples.

You're going to have ones that might not be listed above. That's okay. Write down 20, narrow it down to three, and then get very specific with the three. You want to be specific so you know this woman possesses what you're looking for! Let's say, for example, that you want a woman who's financially responsible. A good indicator of that might be her credit card debt. Okay, that's a good start. But let's get more specific, because 100 dollars in credit debt is quite different than 10,000 dollars in credit card debt. So maybe you come to the conclusion that you don't want a woman who's more than 3,000 dollars in credit card debt. Great, you have something specific. Now you can know for sure she possesses the quality you're looking for. Now, this is a pretty extreme example, so let's try some other ones.

Maybe you want a woman who's an entrepreneur. Well, do you want her to have a new business or one that she's been running for a while? There's a big difference between the two, because in one instance, she's struggling and strapped for time, and in the other, maybe she has lots of free time because she's been running it successfully for 10 years. What's more important to you?

What about being physically fit? What does that look like to you? My version of being physically fit might be night and day compared to yours. To get an idea of what you want, imagine what a physically fit woman looks like. Be careful, though, because you could get caught in a trap of being too picky, which makes this process harder. If you want a woman with big breasts, flat stomach, toned thighs, toned arms, and a big butt, then you're pushing it too far. Why not pick one area that's most important to you and zone in on that. I'm not saying you can't have it all, but be reasonable in your search or it may take forever.

How about similar political beliefs? There's a wide array of beliefs and values, depending on your political system, so which part of politics is most important to you? For example, just saying you want her to be a Democrat might not be enough. Maybe there's something more specific you're looking for, like her belief in pro-life or pro-choice. At that point, it's not really about the full political party but a specific political belief.

Do you see what I'm getting at here? Yes, it can be challenging, but the more specific you are, the better the odds of finding a woman that's right for you. And when you find her, the relationship will have a better chance of succeeding.

Furthermore, you'll want to determine how important your non-negotiables are to you. For example, let's say you are dating a woman who's physically fit, really enthusiastic about having children, and interested in personal development. Then, over time, you find out that she's very religious which you aren't. At this point, maybe you realize that you'd rather be with someone non-religious or the same religion as you. Maybe you would like to have that way more than being into personal development. Boom! Now you've discovered a new, more important non-negotiable: similar religious beliefs. And that has now replaced your non-negotiable of her being into personal development.

So if you narrow your list of 20 qualities down to five or six and you're having a really hard time coming down to three, mix and match the qualities to play out the scenario in your head. Really focus on which ones would make the most difference in your life. You'll be surprised when you realize which ones have the most effect on you and which ones don't.

FIGURING OUT IF SHE HAS THE 3 NON-NEGOTIABLES

Ideally, you want to be doing this as quickly as possible so you don't waste any time. Once you know what you're looking for in a partner, why settle for anything less? This is what dates are for. They give you the opportunity to get to know someone. On a date, you can casually ask her questions that give you the answers you're looking for. Sometimes, she'll just bring them up without you even having to ask. For example, if you're looking for a woman that has a passion, then she might be talking about it nonstop on the first date. Or you can ask her what she's passionate about.

You can even tell her about yourself, and usually a woman will respond and tell you her thoughts on the topic. For example, you could tell her you're excited to have a family one day. She may respond and say something similar, or you can ask her about her opinions after you're done telling her your thoughts.

Now, some topics might be tougher to bring up, like political views, religious views, or financial debt. Don't overthink it and just ask her the questions when it feels appropriate on the first or second date. Why not, right? You might as well find out now so you don't waste time. Can you imagine how difficult it would be if you went on three to six dates and had amazing sex and great conversation but found out she doesn't possess one of your three non-negotiables? You'd probably continue dating her, put aside your non-negotiables, and eventually see problems come out later. And this can lead to years of wasted time and even a potentially nasty divorce if it gets to marriage. If you're trying to get into a strong, long-lasting, monogamous relationship, I urge you to find out if your date has these three non-negotiables as quickly as possible.

HOW TO ASK HER TO BE YOUR GIRLFRIEND

For a monogamous or non-relationship, you're not required to communicate what you're looking for unless she asks. Instead, just continue the courting process by either getting to know her and spending time with her to lead to a relationship (monogamy) or spend infrequent time with her if you're just looking for a sex buddy. For more complicated relationships like threesomes or poly, you must communicate your intentions early so everyone is on the same page.

If you find you've been enjoying spending time with a woman who has your three non-negotiables, then you can ask her to be your girlfriend. My recommendation is that you spend at least three or four months with this person before you commit to a monogamous relationship. Over the course of those months, it's important to get to know her and see what she's like in all different emotional settings. That way, you can know if she'll be a good partner. Ask yourself questions like the ones below:

Does she handle conflict well or does she yell and scream?
Does she handle stress well or does she self-destruct and shy away from her problems?
Does she act respectfully to your friends? To you?
Does she manage her time well or does she live a messy life?
Does she have any mental illnesses she's not in control of?
Does she have any addictions she's not in control of?
Is she independent or clingy?

Those are some questions to think about before you decide to commit to a woman. Make sure you have a rational, respectful, and self-sustaining girlfriend. If she's irrational, mean, or dependent, she'll cause a lot of problems down the road for your relationship. You might be asking, "But, Tripp, she may have some issues but otherwise she's perfect!"

Any issues or red flags you're choosing to ignore now will come up later on in the relationship, and you'll have to deal with them. And it won't be fun. Be smart and make a good choice about who you want to commit to.

If you find an amazing partner, getting her to be your girlfriend is as simple as asking. Ideally, over the course of the past three or four months, you've had enjoyable times together. She'll want to be your girlfriend if you continue practicing tension, entertainment, and dominance in the dating relationship. Here's what that looks like:

Tension: You're consistently having great sex that pleases both of you. Any physicality between you two is very comfortable. You look her in the eyes when you talk to her. You playfully tease her when you're hanging out.

Entertainment: You discuss and talk about things that interest you. You try and keep a positive outlook on life so you can transfer that state to her. You bring her into your world by showing her what interests you, and from time to time, you make her a part of that.

Dominance: You're consistently leading the dating relationship by asking her on dates and planning fun things to do together. You're not afraid to speak your mind and ask for what you want.

Meanwhile, if you're displaying TED and she's a pleasure to be around and suits you as a good partner, ask her to be your girlfriend by saying something like this:

"I really enjoy spending time with you and I don't want to spend time with any other women right now. How do you feel about that?"

This can lead to a discussion about what a monogamous relationship would look like between you two, and you can take it from there.

Remember, never settle for anything that's not the best match for you. If, down the line, it doesn't work out, end it as gracefully as possible and know you can find another match around the corner.

ACTION STEPS:

Think about what type of relationship you're interested in and keep that as your end goal until you change your mind.

Write out 15–20 non-negotiables and narrow it down to the three most important.

CHAPTER 9

PUTTING IT ALL TOGETHER

N ow that you've learned the truth about attraction, how do you put it all together and make it work for you? First, let's go over some of the main concepts you've learned thus far.

Chapter 1

- Triggering attraction comes from displaying your personality and exhibiting masculine traits (inner qualities).

- Attraction is an emotional reaction and not a logical one, which means she doesn't have a choice of whether she's attracted to you or not.

- We use tension (T), entertainment (E), and dominance (D) to effectively trigger attraction and display our masculine traits.

- The two most unattractive traits are neediness and predictability, so avoid both at all costs.

Chapter 2

- Optimizing your outer qualities (wealth, health, lifestyle, and appearance) should be done for you, not for her.

- Each outer quality indirectly benefits your dating life (more access to women, superficial confidence, and creating a healthy emotional state).

- Confidence comes from competence because it's something you do, not something you have.

- Approach anxiety is defeated with systematic desensitization (approaching is a must, and use baby steps to conquer it).

Chapter 3

- For a woman to want to see you again, she must be attracted and invested in you.

- Investment occurs when you spend time with a woman so she can get to know you better.

- To create interesting and easy-flowing conversation, use "Chick Crack: The Topics of Conversation Women Love": http://www.trippadvice. com/chick-crack/.

- To make a conversation continue, use the extraction method to make a statement or ask a question based on what she says.

- Use one or two questions from the 36 questions study to connect more deeply with a woman.

Chapter 4

- You know a woman is interested in you when she's paying attention to you with her body language and verbal clues.

- To lead the interaction, you need to give compliance tests, which get her saying yes all the way to sex.

- If she can't come back to your place, get her number for a future date.

Chapter 5

- Achieving abundance mentality is your most important skill in meeting women; there are plenty of quality women to be with, and there's no need to ever get hung up on just one.

- Never give a woman your number—only get hers by telling her, not asking.

- Use texting for logistics (asking her out), not for building attraction.

- The best first date involves a drink/coffee/tea or some sort of activity.

Chapter 6

- Women love sex just as much as men, but they don't want to be shamed for it.

- The date is identical to the initial interaction: triggering attraction, getting her invested, and leading her to sex.

- Lead the woman from the date to your place by telling her to come over for a glass of wine or by saying you want to show her something you referenced in a previous conversation.

- For your safety and hers, wear a condom and ask for consent before having sex.

Chapter 7

- To go for the kiss, create a silence, then go for it.

- To get a woman turned on, build tension by going slowly and teasing her. Get "Tripp's Tension Technique" for a live video demonstration: http://www.trippadvice.com/tension-technique.

- Learning how to make a girl squirt can open up a woman's sexual world and have her coming back for more.

- Watching porn is a great way to learn about how to perform specific sexual moves and open up your world to new fetishes.

Chapter 8

- There are many different types of relationships. Find out which one best suits you and figure out how to get that type of relationship.

- For a monogamous relationship, determine your three non-negotiables so you end up in a relationship with someone who's your best match.

- Specificity is key in creating your three non-negotiables so you know exactly what to look for when dating multiple women.

- Don't commit to a monogamous relationship until you've been dating consistently for at least three or four months and you find you get along with her well.

HOW TO GET GOOD WITH WOMEN FAST!

With all this information, what are you supposed to do now? For many, it can get overwhelming, so let me teach you how to best learn this material now that you've given the book a first run-through.

Your best course of action *is* action. All this theory and technique is garbage unless you go out and use it. Here's my simple formula for getting good fast:

Speed of Implementation + Get Questions Answered (REPEAT)

Speed of Implementation

Do *not* wait until you have theory and techniques memorized in your head. You should immediately go out and start approaching women. Yes, you'll screw up, and it'll happen a lot. Yes, you're going to get nervous. Yes, you're going to get rejected. So why go out and do it before you're super prepared? Well, first, you'll never be super prepared. You can study this book all day and it won't help. You learn by doing. When you go out and talk to women, you want experience. This experience is what gets you to the next step.

There is no such thing as a good or bad night out. Don't be outcome-dependent. Every time you go out and practice talking to women, you'll inevitably learn *something*. You need to motivate yourself and push hard to get yourself out there. It's like practicing the guitar. How long would you take reading the theory and techniques of playing? Probably not much, right? You'd want to pick up a guitar and start playing away! The same goes with meeting women. Get out there immediately, make mistakes, adopt the abundance mindset, and repeat.

Get Questions Answered

You get better by asking the right questions. Once you start talking to women, the questions will come flooding in:

I wasn't able to approach any women today due to fear. How do I manage approach anxiety?

After I approached, I couldn't continue a conversation. What's the best way to do that?

I went up to 10 women and each one rejected me immediately. Am I using a good opener?

I got three phone numbers today, but none have texted me back. What can I do to fix that?

I tried to bounce a woman back to my place, but she said she had work in the morning. What's my next move?

All those questions and more will start shooting through your brain as you're approaching and implementing. You can use this book as your reference guide to answer all the above questions and more. So the idea is to go out, talk to women, identify where you're having trouble, ask the question, and seek the answer. Then you go out, use the new information, and apply it. Repeat this process over and over and over.

THE 3 THINGS STOPPING YOU FROM TAKING ACTION

Most of the time, one of two things stops my clients from taking action: fear, time and motivation.

Fear

Yes, I understand that approaching women can be scary, and it takes a lot of strength to push yourself to go up and say hi. Let me fast-forward your life for a second.

Imagine a world in which you had the ability to attract one of the hottest women at a party. You knew how to start the conversation, get things flowing, attract her, and bring her home that night. The next night, you have a date set up with a woman you met at a coffee shop one week earlier. She was that cute, green-eyed brunette sipping her latte. The upcoming weekend, you're going out on a yacht with a new friend you met one night while out socializing. In fact, he's grateful to you because you introduced him to multiple hot girls at a club one night. This guy is very connected, so you know you'll meet some hot women and get some good networking opportunities. Your social life is in abundance.

That picture I created for you isn't a dream. This can easily be your reality. All it takes is leaving your house and opening your mouth. The opportunity of adventure is endless if you take action and meet people. It's the difference between putting yourself out there and not. For motivation, picture the life you want, then reread the approach anxiety section in Chapter 2 and start your journey.

Motivation

One of the biggest lessons I've learned in my life is that anything worth having takes work. That's the bottom line and I don't know how to sugar coat it. Life is hard. Getting the things you want is hard. We fall many times before we learn how to ride our bike. So how do we motivate ourselves to keep going?

The first night I went out to soberly approach women I had a very tough time. I spent 3 hours getting the courage to simply say "hi" to a girl. And I couldn't even do it. When I went home that night I immediately wanted to quit. But then I thought long and hard about my options and it boiled down to two:

1) Go out and keep trying to talk to women and tough it out
2) Not go out and stay inside my loneliness bubble forever

The worst case scenario would be that both options lead me to the same place: alone or settling with a girl I don't want. But that wasn't a guarantee. There was still a chance I could learn this stuff and be able to date great women! So what's the worst that could happen? Nothing. I would still be exactly where I am. This motivated me to keep going and I'm glad I did because now I get to share my wisdom with you.

Another way to find motivation is to find your "why". Why are you doing this? Why are you reading this book? What is it that you want? What is your desire? Answer that to yourself right now. Better yet, write it down somewhere and keep it on you at all times. Then refer to it when you are having bad nights out or feel down in the dumps. There must be some spark inside of you that wants to change and have the women of your choice. What's your "why"?

Time

Now, I know some men have issues with time. You may have a busy schedule with work, studying, hanging out with current friends, doing hobbies, or more. Let me say that, no matter how busy your life currently is, you can always make room for something that's a priority. If you want this badly enough, there's always an hour or 10 that you can squeeze into a week without a problem.

If it's work or school you're busy with, I recommend taking a hard look at your schedule and squeezing in 30 minutes to an hour of time to go out and approach. This can be during lunch, after work, on the weekends, during your errands run, or even while you're participating in your current hobby. There's always an hour you can sneak in. Always. And if you're still saying there isn't, then be more aggressive with how you spend your time.

If you spend a lot of time with your friends, turn them on to this book and go out together. If they aren't interested in meeting women, sacrifice time with them, do something special for you, and get approaching. If you have a lot of hobbies, maybe it's time to make this a new hobby and put aside an old one for now. If your work gets you home late on weekdays, spend more time approaching on the weekend.

We all have excuses and can easily just walk away from something that's challenging. Your brain is good at playing the victim and saying "woe is me." And you can sit in your comfortable life and always wonder "what if?" What if I tried to meet more women? What if I ended up with a hot woman in my bed this weekend? What if I met the woman of my dreams from a random approach in a grocery store? What if I made a bunch of new, high-quality friends that made life more fun? What if?

As a guy, just like you, who went through this same process, I can tell you it's worth it.

To make this simple, I'm going to give you Tripp's 30-Day Challenge. This is something you can do to kickstart the process of approaching women and *doing* confidence.

Tripp's 30-Day Challenge
1. Go out for a minimum of 30 minutes per day
2. No apologizing or explaining yourself
3. Dress your best
4. Collect 10 cans or bottles
5. Meditate for five minutes per day

The challenge is to accomplish all five tasks every day for 30 straight days. This begins building habits that'll directly and indirectly help you get good at meeting women. And you can start as soon as today.

Go Out for a Minimum of 30 Minutes Per Day

In these 30 minutes, do as many approaches as you can. This can be at night or during the day; it's your call. I'd start a timer on your phone or watch and jump right into it. Make it a game for yourself and see how many approaches you can do in this given time. Don't discriminate, either. If you only wait to talk to girls you're attracted to, then this will be a long process. Whether you're on the sidewalk or at a nightclub, talk to everyone. Get yourself into a social mood. Every single approach is a learning experience.

No Apologizing or Explaining Yourself

Don't apologize for doing what you're doing. And don't feel you have to explain yourself for your actions. You'll catch yourself doing this a lot, and this is "nice guy" mentality. Busting this habit will help you get out of your head and help you stop caring what people think. Remember, this is your journey and your growth period. This has nothing to do with anyone but *you*. Also, not having to apologize for your actions helps you speak in the affirmative (downward tonality). You'll come across as more dominant in your interactions.

Dress Your Best

This is going to accomplish a few things: discipline and superficial confidence. Having to dress your best every day is challenging. It takes a lot of work to look your best. This disciplinary action makes you mentally stronger because of the effort it requires. My advice is to figure out the night before what you'll wear and execute it the next day. Dressing well will also give you a mental boost for the day. It creates a mindset of preparedness to take on the day. Lastly, it'll optimize your physical appearance for your approaches.

Collect 10 Cans and Bottles

This is another disciplinary action that's challenging to accomplish every day; thus, it makes you mentally stronger. It's also a good thing to do for the environment, which will give you a mental boost and a sense of accomplishment. Also, you may not find cans and bottles just lying in the street. My recommendation is to find people who are almost about to finish theirs. Tell them you'll recycle it for them. Yup, this might be scary. Good! It'll force you out of your comfort zone and help you practice approaching. Note that this is not part of your 30 minutes of going out.

Meditate for Five Minutes Per Day

I would download an app on your phone for this. My recommendation is Headspace. At the very least, time yourself for five minutes and sit comfortably and just focus on your breathing. Every time a thought enters your brain, notice it but then come back to your breathing. This daily exercise will help form a habit to quiet the noise in your brain and relax. You can do this before or after you go out for your 30 minutes. It'll train you to be more present and relaxed in your interactions.

This 30-day challenge is exactly what it says it is: challenging. I suggest you do this right away. Start today or tomorrow at the latest. Don't worry about doing everything perfectly. What's important is creating habits. You're going to mess up for the first three to five days. You might not end up approaching anyone for the 30 minutes you're out. You may only collect six cans and bottles. The nicest pair of clothes you own might be jeans and a T-shirt. That's fine. Don't wait to start this process. Think "progress over perfection." If you keep up with this for 30 days, I bet you'll nail it in your last week. And by the end of the challenge, a crazy little thing happens: you're going to feel good about yourself. This is called self-esteem, and it's crucial to becoming magnetic.

I also recommend using the journal at the end of this book to take notes on your daily progress through the 30-day challenge. You'll see a section called "notes," where I encourage you to write what you did well and what needs improvement. That way, you can progress through the challenge and be consciously aware of how to keep improving.

HOW TO BECOME MAGNETIC

Famous biologist Charles Darwin said, "It is not the strongest of the species that survive, nor the most intelligent, but the one most responsive to change."

If you commit to making a change in your life and take on the tasks and practices I've discussed, there's nowhere to go but up. Your mission, if you so choose it, is growth and change. Not everyone is cut out for this kind of work, and if it were easy, everyone would be doing it. But change and growth come from the desire to go after what you want and the drive to persevere. Some days will be great, and some days will be terrible. Consistency is what breeds success.

So when times get tough, ask yourself this question:

How bad do I want this?

If your answer is "not that much," maybe this isn't for you. Not everyone can succeed in the area of women and dating. That's just reality. Life will cut out the ones that aren't the most *responsive to change*.

However, I recommend you take this journey if you know you want to be the guy that can do any of this:

• confidently walk into any room and get people's attention
• attract and sleep with women "out of your league"
• find the exact relationship you desire
• defeat the painful anxiety and shyness inside your chest
• feel comfortable inside your own skin

The only difference between the "old" you and the future, magnetic you is putting in the work. And it's all laid out for you here. The map is in your hands. Now it's time to follow it. Take full control of your life and join me and thousands of others who did the same.

Are you ready?

Time to get to work.

BONUS CHAPTER:

I CAN'T GET IT UP! (HOW TO FIX ERECTILE DYSFUNCTION FAST AND NATURALLY)

There comes a time in every man's life when he fails to get an erection. It's happened to me. It's happened to my friends. It's happened to my clients. Maybe it's even happened to you. It can be very frustrating and destroy a man's confidence in the bedroom. What you have to understand is that it's completely normal and it's not your fault. Well, it's a little your fault. There might be something you're doing that's preventing you from getting an erection when the time is right. In this chapter, let's take a look at a few things you might be doing and how to fix them so you can significantly reduce the chances of erectile dysfunction. I'm a big believer in doing things naturally so you don't have to rely on pills. What follows are natural tips for a more sustainable solution to this problem instead of relying on pharmaceuticals.

Masturbating Too Much to Pornography or in General

It's hard to say what's "too much" because everyone has a different sex drive, but if you think you're masturbating too much or watching too much porn, then it might be time to try and cut back. My advice to you is to cut whatever you're doing now in half. This will re-sensitize you to sex and sexual situations. Many men might find it difficult to get an erection because the woman they're with doesn't "compare" to the women in porn. Or they've already masturbated 10 times that week and their body isn't as responsive to a sexual situation.

Cut down on pleasing yourself and save it for when you're with a woman. Some men even do "no fap," which is an Internet term for no masturbating. As a challenge, I suggest you try it for two or three weeks and see what it does to your body. You might find that it reinvigorates your sex drive and gives you erections when you aren't even looking for them.

Meditation

One of the most common reasons for erectile dysfunction is stress and anxiety. A man will be with a woman and be so inside of his mind that his body isn't responding to what's happening in front of him. A great way to get out of your head and into your body is to practice meditation. If you're in the middle of Tripp's 30-Day Challenge, this should be a regular part of your regimen. Five minutes of meditation per day can make you more aware of what's happening in the moment. It takes a minute to get comfortable with meditation, which is why you should start as soon as possible.

Also, when you're with a woman, take your time. Going slowly is a great way to not only turn her on, but also turn you on. When you're getting intimate with her, there's no need to rush. Explore her body slowly and be present to all the feelings in yours. This will help you relax and get into the present state, which hopefully is lust and desire.

Be Conscious of What You're Putting in Your Body

What you're eating, ingesting, or smoking can have a big effect on the way your body operates. You might be taking medication that has a side effect of low libido. Talk to your doctor about the medications you're on. If you're a big drinker, smoker, or drug user, this can also affect the way your body responds to sex. If you've ever had too much to drink one night, you already know what happens when you're with a woman and about to get intimate: things go limp. Be mindful of what you're putting in your body and take a realistic look at your drug and alcohol habits.

Eating healthy is also a big factor in how your body works. If you're eating fast food every day and not putting any nutrition inside your body, you can't function at optimal levels. My advice is to start replacing low-nutritional foods with greens. See Chapter 2 for my Green Monster drink recipe to get you started. You can also use ginseng and maca root in a smoothie. They've both been known to help with erectile dysfunction.

Get Your Bloodwork Done

A common but often overlooked issue with erectile dysfunction is low testosterone. Whether you're getting older or have a deficiency, this could be causing the problem. Go to your doctor and get your bloodwork done to check for low testosterone. If you find you're not producing enough testosterone, try to cure it naturally with zinc, vitamin D, more sleep, and exercise. Your doctor may want to prescribe pills, but stick to a natural plan first, because you may be surprised with the results.

Get Physical

Getting to the gym a few times a week or doing aerobic activity is great for your body and testosterone levels. I recommend putting a quick workout plan together to start being more active. Your body is a temple, and it's in control of giving you harder erections and getting you turned on. So treat it well and you should hopefully see some results down there.

QUICK-STEP ACTION PLAN

You have some ideas of what might be causing erectile dysfunction and maybe you had a couple of ah-ha moments as you were reading about what causes it. Now it's time to put a plan into action so you know what to do and don't get overwhelmed. Here's what you can start doing this week:

- Cut down the number of times you masturbate per week by half.
- Cut down on cigarette, alcohol, and drug use to create a healthier response in your body to sex.
- Buy leafy green vegetables, green powder, maca root, zinc, vitamin D, and ginseng at the store. Mix the powders in your morning green smoothie and take the vitamins after breakfast or as prescribed.
- Get a gym membership and start working out two or three times per week, including a few days for cardio.
- Download a meditation app on your phone and start a daily five-minute meditation routine for relaxation and awareness
- If the above steps don't help, get your bloodwork done at a doctor and test for low testosterone levels.

— ∼ —

NOTES

notes

notes

Made in the USA
Las Vegas, NV
30 January 2024

85090195R00105